Gut Feelings:
Coping With Cancer
and Living With Lynch Syndrome

Sam Rose

ISBN: 9798581399507
www.writersam.co.uk
twitter.com/writersamr
Copyright © Sam Rose 2021
Peeking Cat Literary

Contents

Foreword

I began writing this memoir in 2019, a few months after my second and third major cancer surgeries. If I were beginning writing the memoir now, at the end of 2020, this would be a very different book.

My cancer experiences have had such an impact on me that I'm now doing a PhD on them. In October 2019 I started my PhD at Teesside University, researching the connection between creative writing and the emotional aspects of cancer survivorship. Over a year into my research, I have been thinking about – and writing about – cancer survivorship issues even more than usual, and I could have added a lot more to this book based on the papers and journals I have been reading. However, I think it is important to preserve the thoughts I wrote down just a few months after surgery, rather than bury them in academic research. I would like this book to be useful for people who have been where I was and still am. If you or someone you are close to is facing cancer, surgeries, or Lynch syndrome, I would love for you to find something in these pages that you can relate to or that helps you, whether you're just starting to navigate this world or you're a seasoned expert like me.

This book is split into two parts. Part one: Large Intestine is my cancer story, from my first diagnosis in 2010 to the aftermath of my most recent surgery at the time of writing, in 2019. Part Two: Small Intestine is a reflection on why cancer is traumatic, how this manifests itself, the physical and emotional difficulties that cancer survivors can face, and some self-care ideas for cancer survivors.

If you'd like to get in touch after reading this, my virtual door is open. Visit writersam.co.uk or email me at writer.sam@outlook.com. Let's chat.

Part One
The Large Intestine

Chapter One
I Haven't Got the Guts For This

How many organs do you have? I get so mixed up when I try to count mine. I imagine my body as a bit like one of those scratch-off maps – you know, the ones where you take a coin and scratch off the foil over all the countries you've been to, revealing the green countries underneath, and it hangs on your wall as a kind of record of travel achievement. Except mine would be a map of my body and I'd scratch off all the organs that have been removed. I don't want to spoil the story too much for you right away, but if I were to make a shopping list of my bloody bits that are sitting in jars somewhere, being dissected, or have otherwise been discarded as medical waste, it would look something like this:

- Large intestine
- Appendix
- Uterus
- Ovaries
- Fallopian tubes
- Duodenum
- Pancreas (head of)
- Gallbladder
- Bile duct

According to my research, not everyone agrees on how many organs are in the human body, and it's unclear what definitely counts as an organ and what doesn't. But if we go by the commonly stated figure of 78, that's about 12% of my body map I'd be able to scratch off. It's not all bad, though – as my partner Peter always says, it just means there's less of me to go wrong. After having cancer three times by the time I was thirty, I would hope that the remaining organs have been watching what's been happening to their sisters, and they will keep in line from now on. I can tell where my organs are missing, so maybe they can, too. I mean it – if I put a hand on each side of my waist and push in a little, I can feel a gap at my right-hand side where things are a bit less crowded. I have decided to make that a fact that I like about myself. But it isn't always easy to spin trauma into interesting or even positive personal traits.

I've written horror stories before but some of the events from this memoir scare me more than any paranormal activity I've ever imagined. It was January 2010 when my cancer experience was kick-started. I say "experience" because "journey" sounds like I'm going on a bit of a jolly, and "battle" makes it sound like the patient can get rid of their cancer if they try hard enough. That would be nice, wouldn't it? The only thing I was "battling" in January 2010 was the snow. I was 22 years old and working at Sainsbury's part-time. I'd graduated from the University of Northampton with an IT degree the previous summer, but I hadn't yet found a full-time job that would enable me to put that degree to good use. I was picky about the jobs I applied for – partly because I was a bit scared about starting somewhere new, so I wanted the job I chose to be perfect. It's probably also reasonable to blame the 2008 financial crisis for a lack of appropriate jobs. That's why in early

January 2010 I was still working twelve hours per week in a cliquey shop where I didn't have any friends and I was quite keen to leave. I was happy to be working part-time and have all of this free time to do whatever I wanted, like going to the gym during the day when the pool was almost empty. Or working on the literary magazine I edited, pages of poems strewn across the living room floor. Or spending time with my friends or with Peter. I did want to get a full-time job, but the thought of starting somewhere new was scary. What if the people weren't nice and I didn't make friends, or I couldn't do the work, or I hated it, or the commute was too long? I only wanted to apply for jobs I felt completely comfortable with applying for – and that narrowed things down quite a bit. So I was still working at the supermarket, which wasn't all bad. It was nice at Christmas when everyone was busy and cheerful, at least. But now the January blues had officially set in and the weather wasn't helping.

One night, my dad met me at work and walked me home, as I wasn't so keen on walking by myself in the ice and snow late in the evening. It was bitterly cold and I was bundled up in my scarf and gloves and trying not to slip. When we got inside I made myself a hot chocolate and eventually retired to my bedroom, but not to sleep. With no need to get up early most mornings, I spent my nights watching my favourite shows on DVD and playing on my Xbox 360 – that night Guitar Hero was my game of choice. Quietly, though, as my parents were in bed and I usually didn't go to sleep myself until around 2am.

This is where it gets a bit gross. But this is basically a memoir about my insides – the biological kind and the emotional kind – so we'll start as we mean to go on. I'm certainly past the point of being squeamish. I had been having some trouble for a little while with what I assumed was haemorrhoids. There would be a little blood on the paper when I went to the toilet. But that night, when I turned off my console and started getting ready for bed, I went to the toilet and I wouldn't stop bleeding. I was on my period so it was difficult to tell how much blood was coming from where, but I knew it wasn't right. I wiped, and there was still blood. Wiped again, still more blood. It felt as if something inside had popped its little head out of my bum (as it had done before), but this time it wouldn't go back in, and that was the source of the blood. It was something round in shape, a lump that shouldn't have been there. I was freaked out and didn't know what to do, but I didn't want to wake up my parents, so I went to bed anyway and hoped it would stop bleeding on its own. Of course, I couldn't sleep. I kept getting up to check on it, and it hadn't improved. At around five in the morning, I went downstairs, turned on my laptop and tried Googling the problem to figure out what was going on (this was before I had a mobile phone I could use the internet on). I couldn't find anything online that sounded like my problem. I went back to bed to continue the worrying and intermittent sleeping. When morning finally came I went into my parents' bedroom to wake them up and tell them I needed to go to the doctor.

I went into the doctor's office with my mum while my dad waited for us in the car. Dr Datta was nice, but very chatty, which may have been why her clinic was always overrunning.

"Right, let me take a look," she said and pulled the curtains around the bed. I pulled my jeans down a little and laid down to let her see. She seemed a little fascinated with it.

"Ooh, yes, how strange," Dr Datta said. "I don't think that is piles. I'm not sure what it is. I think you should go to A&E to get it checked out."

Cue panic. I had never been to the hospital for myself before, and I felt like it would be the scariest place I could possibly go to, except for prison. The doctor told me and my mum that she would write a letter I could give in at the hospital to say that she had referred me there. I sat impatiently as she sorted out the letter then paused to talk about how the snow had caused problems in the car park that morning. *Come on*, I thought. My problem was obviously more important. Didn't she have any sense of urgency?

My mum and I walked back to the car. "We have to go to the hospital," I said. Dad looked up in surprise.

"What, now?"

"Yeah, we have to go to A&E now."

So Dad drove us to the hospital, my stomach doing somersaults all the way there. I handed in my letter. After a few minutes, a nurse called me into a room to discuss the problem. I asked her for a sanitary towel because I hadn't brought any with me – not expecting to end up at the hospital – and the thing was still bleeding. On top of feeling anxious about this thing and what was happening to me, I was worried about not having any pads and blood seeping through to my jeans. We sat in the waiting room for a while, and eventually, I was called in to see someone else. Whoever he was, he took a look at "the thing" as well and gave me a general check-up.

"Has anyone ever said you have a heart murmur?" he asked after brandishing his stethoscope.

"No," I said, completely puzzled. My mother just laughed – I guess out of nervousness because I was so terrified I had no idea what could have been so funny. And what was this man going on about, a heart murmur? Did he know what he was doing? It was a very peculiar thing to say, because he didn't say anything else about it, and nobody ever mentioned anything like it afterwards.

After seeing him, we went back into the waiting room. I hadn't had any breakfast so my dad bought me a packet of crisps out of the vending machine. This displeased the two porters who eventually came to collect me to take me upstairs since if I needed an operation I shouldn't have been eating beforehand. You have to be nil by mouth before an operation because the anaesthetic stops your body's reflexes and if you have food or drink in your stomach, you might throw up and end up with food in your lungs – which isn't where you want it to be, obviously. Well, now we know. Now we know so much more about the medical world. I feel like it's made me a completely different person – how happily ignorant I was about everything before this day in January 2010, and how lucky other people are if they have never needed to know any of this. I sometimes wonder what that must be like, to not have these medical issues to worry about. I feel like if I was suddenly told that I was perfectly healthy and didn't have to be under surveillance for any problems, I would be grateful every single day.

The two porters took me upstairs in a wheelchair, which my father and I both protested as unnecessary. I got in the chair and already felt like there was something wrong with me – why wasn't I even allowed to walk anymore? What was so wrong with me that I wasn't allowed to walk, but not wrong enough for me to really feel unwell?

Once I had a bed on the A&E ward, I was seen by a doctor who checked me out. He was the third person of the day I showed my butt to, but I think he was the first one to stick his finger up there – and in front of a nurse, as well.

"Is this the highlight of your day?" I asked as I felt the slight discomfort of his gloved finger. "Because it's the highlight of mine."

He laughed, and I felt like I was in good hands (or I had good hands in me, I suppose). He was about thirty, a little round, with glasses and a good-natured smile. He seemed quite laid back and made me feel a little more at ease.

"That is a polyp," he said with confidence, once I was decent again. I was no wiser.

"What's a polyp?" I asked.

"It's a little growth, sort of like a wart."

So that was that mystery solved. However, I had lost quite a bit of blood so I needed a transfusion. I was in for an overnight stay so that four pints of blood could be poured back into me. That's about half of the blood I should have in my body. My parents disappeared and came back with some magazines and puzzle books to keep me occupied. Later, I was moved from A&E to a regular ward and a nurse offered me some toast since it was late by that time and I had missed dinner. I remember being surprised and delighted at what I saw as a very kind gesture. Now I've had more hospital experience, I don't know why I felt so touched by toast, as of course, it's normal to be given food while you're in hospital. Perhaps it was because I had never been looked after by a stranger before.

Because I was having a blood transfusion I was given something else through IV so I wouldn't get "overloaded". I wasn't sure what it was but when they said it would make me need to pee a lot, they weren't kidding. I spent half the night trundling up and down the otherwise quiet corridor, taking my IV drip stand for a walk to the toilet and back again, under the sympathetic eyes of the nurses. I would come back to bed and then immediately need to go again, and it got so bad that eventually, I went once, then hung around in the bathroom for two minutes until the urge returned. What was the point in going back to bed? Pair that with being woken up throughout the night anyway to have my blood pressure taken, and it was another bad night's sleep.

I was fascinated by the effects of the blood transfusion, though. I have always been a bit pasty and even had a customer at work offer for her sister, who was a nurse, to give me a blood test. (I declined.) Looking in the mirror during one of my many bathroom visits, I could see the colour returning to my cheeks, lips and hands. My hands looked like I'd been stood out in the cold, and my lips were pinker than they had ever looked. I felt like I had stolen them from Snow White – I had given her back her ivory skin and taken her rosy red lips. Standing in that clinical, very alien-feeling toilet, I felt alone and out of place, but my pink skin brought me a small spark of joy. Or perhaps I am remembering things a little too fondly. I do wonder if my brain tries to protect me from remembering the reality of these things.

I was woken up in the morning by a nurse opening the curtains to reveal the bright 8am sunshine, and it was toast again for breakfast. Mr Rashed, the bowel surgeon who would become my consultant for the next ten years and counting, came to examine me a couple of hours later. He asked if he could stick his finger in my bottom (didn't I feel popular?) and proceeded to do so with several of his entourage watching, at which point I almost died of embarrassment. I suppose I could have said no. Needless to say, I haven't seen my dignity since, but I'm sure it was just a burden anyway and I'm better off without it. What good has embarrassment ever done me?

Luckily the bleeding had stopped at some point during the previous afternoon and I could go home, but I was going home with something missing (besides my dignity). When I was getting ready to go to the doctor's surgery I had stood in my bedroom looking at the pile of clothes on the floor, and I had wondered if I should take my scarf. It was more of a pashmina, and it was absolutely beautiful. I had chosen it myself as a Christmas present from my parents a year or two before. It was long and wide and made up of brightly coloured squares. Each one had its own pattern such as stripes or paisley, and it glittered silver in places. It was well-made and stunning, and I loved it. Which is why I wish I hadn't decided to bring it with me, because somewhere between being in A&E and my parents taking my things to the car that day, it had gotten lost. Calls to the hospital in the days afterwards to see if it was in their lost and found box yielded nothing. Someone else was enjoying my scarf now, and whoever they were I hated them for it. I still miss it. I know it is probably a symbol for the entire experience now, as well as simply being a beautiful accessory. It was one of the first things cancer made me lose. Well, that any my dignity. I don't particularly miss that.

I had to get the polyp removed, so I spent the next few weeks waiting for a date to come through, worrying about it, dreading going to the toilet in case I started bleeding again, and generally feeling fed up with my lot in life. My friend Al and I had tickets to see my favourite band at the time, 30 Seconds To Mars, in London in February, and I was worried that any hospital visits could interfere with our plans. I love lots of different kinds of music, but especially rock bands, and especially this one – and especially the adrenaline rush of seeing them perform my favourite songs live, the ones that I can relate to the most. I called Mr Rashed's secretary to find out if there was a date for my operation yet, and she said there wasn't one. "We need to give priority to the cancer patients, you see," she explained. *How do you know I'm not one of them?* I thought, though I wasn't really worried about that as a diagnosis at the time. I just wanted to get the operation over and done with so that I could go back to searching for a job. Get this blip out of the way and go back to normal. I felt like my life was on hold in the meantime and that nothing good was happening. When were things going to start looking up for me? It was time to start being an adult like my friends were. Get a proper job, move out of Mum and Dad's house, and be independent. I didn't need the stress this new world of hospital appointments was bringing. I am a very independent person who is usually happy in her own company, but at that time I didn't want to be alone because I would then think about things and worry. I didn't like this new feeling of wanting company all the time and being too afraid to be on my own, because it wasn't me. I was worried quite a lot of the time and constantly scared to go to the toilet. Every time I went I hoped there wouldn't be blood, and if there was I'd get a sinking feeling in my stomach. I thought if there wasn't blood, maybe the thing was somehow getting better on its own, but it wasn't. Something was not right at all.

I didn't need to worry about the trip to London, as things didn't happen that quickly. Al and I had a great time at the gig, particularly thanks to an eagle-eyed observation of his. When we arrived at Wembley Arena he spotted that there was a second, small stage near the soundbox in the middle of the floor and it had a drum kit stood on it. Certain this was going to be used at some point during the evening, we stood next to the stage, and sure enough halfway through the gig the band members came running past us in the audience and got up on that stage. In a moment of madness I reached out to lead singer and guitarist Jared Leto as he ran past, and my fingers brushed his arm. I would brag about that for several days to come. For the next ten minutes or so we were in the front row while they did a set of songs on the small stage. I had never dared to be in the front row at a gig before, for fear of being crushed or falling over, or simply because I was unable to get there early enough to take the prime spot (and not lose it by needing to go to the bathroom). But this was a great experience, and it felt really special – especially since I figured I wouldn't be at the front for a gig ever again unless we managed to pull the same trick.

The concert also did one other thing for me. When we went inside we had our wrists stamped so we could go in and out of the venue, and it didn't wash off for a couple of days afterwards. There was something about having some unusual ink on my arm that I liked, as I caught surprise glimpses of it throughout the day. And that's when I started to think about getting a tattoo. This could be something good to happen for me – finally, something to look forward to. And something happening to my body that I had control of. Something positive for my body. In April, after never really thinking about it or even particularly liking tattoos before, I got my first – a triangle symbol with "Provehito In Altum" written over the top, meaning "Launch forth into the deep". A 30 Seconds To Mars tattoo, as it was their motto and symbol, but it also had a deeper meaning for me. I wanted it to be my prompt to not be afraid – to do the things I really wanted to do and to be brave and get a job I would love. I reached out to an old school mate who'd gotten tattoos recently and asked for some advice on where to go and what the experience was like. I remember saying that I should probably get the tattoo after my operation because otherwise, I'd need to worry about looking after it while I was in the hospital. I didn't mention what I was going in for and he said "Nothing bad, I hope!" I agreed and said it was just a little thing, nothing to worry about. I didn't know I was wrong.

In mid-April, I had the polyp removed via laparoscopic surgery. It was a small surgery but having never had one before, it was even scarier than going to A&E for the first time. I don't remember too much about my stay in the hospital this time, except for feeling very scared when they wheeled me down to surgery, away from my parents. It really pales in significance compared to what was to come.

The polyp got sent away for tests and in early May I went back to see Mr Rashed to find out if it was benign. The nurse put my parents and me in a room and sat me by a desk, which was empty except for two boxes of tissues. I wondered if the tissues would be there if it was good news. Maybe there is a good news room and a bad news room - a tissue room and a no-tissue room. Mr Rashed came in and started saying things I didn't like the sound of and I wondered what he was building up to. *Just get to the point, already*, I thought. We were all spinning plates waiting to fall. He eventually said that the polyp wasn't benign and that it contained a few cancer cells. They had gotten rid of it of course, but they needed to do a few tests, including taking a ride through a CT scanner. A doughnut-shape thing, the nice male nurse who was sitting in with us said after my consultant left. And an MRI – that claustrophobic tunnel thing. Like on television. Think of fields, wide open spaces. And then a colonoscopy. You know, when they stick a camera on a long tube up your butt. All outpatient stuff. They weren't expecting any surprises. But if you expected it, then it wouldn't be a surprise, would it? But no, it's routine they said. They do it for everybody.

Of course, I was scared. So scared and surprised that it was cancer. But at this point, I was really just going through the motions. I just did what they told me to do, just waited for the appointments and went to them. I met up with friends and tried to have fun in between but again, I don't remember much about it. I remember the appointments and I remember the fear because it's a fear I have felt on and off ever since. When I was going through cancer diagnosis and treatment, every time it felt like who I was had taken a backseat. When I was getting check-ups and seeing consultants, I felt like a patient first and foremost, and everything else that I was didn't really factor in. And the real shock and distress of everything that happened didn't fully descend until much later. It's like being in a constant state of fight or flight – I don't have time to be myself because there is a constant, low-key panic. Even post-treatment there is this feeling, whenever there is a check-up to go to or results to wait for. I can barely remember this being a new feeling.

So I went for a CT scan, an MRI scan, and a colonoscopy. The first two were fine – they were non-invasive and perfectly painless, apart from having a cannula put in my arm to inject some dye during the CT scan. A cannula, for the uninitiated, is a tube you have put into a vein in your hand or arm so that you can be given stuff via IV – like medication or anaesthetic, or dye for a CT scan, or blood during a transfusion, or stuff that makes you pee while you're having a blood transfusion. I would become very well acquainted with cannulas, and grow to hate them quite a lot. It hurt to have them put in, they got in the way while I was trying to do things, and they were uncomfortable, tugging at my hand whenever I moved.

While the scans were easy enough to put up with, the colonoscopy, on the other hand, was awful. I was apparently sedated, but it didn't feel like it. It was one of the most painful things I have ever experienced, partly because during the procedure they have to fill your stomach with air, which is really uncomfortable, like bad stomach cramps. And it seemed to take forever. I remember crying out in pain like I was being tortured. Gripping the nurse's hand really tightly, and then squeezing the metal bed frame instead because I was afraid of hurting her. I've had plenty of similar procedures since then, and none of them were quite that bad. During that colonoscopy I had eighteen more polyps removed. I couldn't feel the polyps being removed in particular, but the whole thing hurt and took so long. The sedation they give during this procedure isn't supposed to make you sleep. It's just supposed to make you feel a bit woozy so that you don't really remember what happened afterwards. But I was in so much pain it didn't feel like it was doing anything for me at all. I should mention that not all colonoscopies are that painful, and it shouldn't put anyone off having one if you need one. We have to do these things to keep ourselves safe, and even if it's unpleasant, it's worth it.

After they were finally done, I went back into the recovery room and everyone else was gone, which meant my parents could come in. I just held my mum's hand and cried – I was so glad that it was over. I felt like I had been broken, physically and mentally. But I rallied around. The colonoscopy was the same day as my nephew's birthday and that same day, my parents and I were at my sister Karen's house for his birthday dinner.

My niece and nephew were around a lot when I was growing up as my mum would often babysit while my sister and her then-husband were at work. My sister is twelve years older than me and got married when I was seven. She had my nephew Brandon when I was ten years old and I remember her bringing him in to see my class in year six because we were talking about babies and reproductive systems. I was so proud to have them there and excited for him to get so much attention. I think he took a particular liking to a boy named Kyle, who also seemed to love him. That was one of the most fun afternoons of my primary school days.

Two years later, Brandon's sister Jade was born. Brandon was at my house when mum got the phone call and repeated the information to me as she received it. I got down on the floor and crawled over to where Brandon was sitting under the dining table. "Your sister is called Jade!" I said, excited because at the time it was my favourite name, and I probably wrote lots of stories with main characters called Jade. "No, she isn't!" Brandon argued. Well, okay then.

Karen got divorced ten years later and is now married to Neil, who has three boys as well as a daughter in Germany. Some of my favourite memories are when my parents and I would go to Karen and Neil's house and we'd all have dinner together with the kids – Brandon and Jade, and Neil's boys Josh, Matt and James. The "kids" are all adults now and it got more difficult to wrangle everyone onto the same room as time went on, but the best nights were those spent in Karen's swimming pool at the barn conversion she lived in for a while, or all gathering around the fire pit in the garden, or digging into Neil's chicken fajitas.

Chapter Two
Absolutely Gutted

Back in 2010, things weren't going any better, as about a month later my mother came into my bedroom to wake me up. She had been crying.

"Bad news," she said, sitting on the edge of my bed.

I looked at her, still bleary-eyed. "Grandad died," I said.

"Yeah," she said. "How did you know?"

"I don't know." I suppose I had figured that she was upset so obviously something had happened to someone, and Grandad had already had eight heart attacks. He'd had nine lives, like a cat.

"He had another heart attack. Your dad drove up to see him, but he got a phone call when he was twenty minutes away from the hospital. He was already gone."

It was Father's Day. My grandparents lived in Greater Manchester, nearly a three-hour drive away from us. My dad stayed up there for a couple of days, and I gave him his Father's Day presents when he got back. Awkward and unsure of what to do with myself. I had never been close with any of my grandparents as I only saw them a couple of times a year, but I was sad for everyone else. Grandad was a wind-up merchant, with a very dry sense of humour so you never knew if he was joking or being serious. I liked him. There is a photograph from when he and my grandmother visited once when I was a kid, and I am tipping my box of Barbie clothes over his head as he sits doing his cryptic crossword. Then there's a second photograph from later that same evening of me eating a chocolate chip muffin – or trying to, until Grandad put his hand over mine holding the muffin and pushed the cake into my face.

A few days after Grandad died, my parents and I were back in the clinic with my consultant. They had sent off some biopsies from my colonoscopy and we were going back for the results. The anxiety of sitting in a hospital waiting room was becoming familiar. When we were finally called into the consultation room, Mr Rashed was there, along with a few other people. That was intimidating – what were they all doing there? I'm not sure I can even express how scary it is to have to go through tests, then get the results, wondering what on earth is happening to your usually perfectly calm life – let alone entering a room with three or four people all looking quite serious – and dealing with all of that at the age of 22. And there was the guilt of putting my parents through whatever we were about to be told. Pointless, irrational, inescapable guilt.

Mr Rashed told me that there were some cancerous cells in the polyps they had removed and that because I was so young and there were so many polyps, I should have my entire bowel removed to prevent anything worse happening in the future. My mother cried. My dad asked Mr Rashed if he was definitely the best man for the job. I was just numb. My large intestine was going to be removed and I was going to have a colostomy. Those were the facts, but I couldn't connect myself with them. Mr Rashed left and we went into a different room to talk to the other people there, who were stoma nurses. My dad kept thinking they were saying "stomach" because we had no idea what a stoma was. They explained that a stoma is a little bit of large intestine that sticks through a hole in the stomach, and waste comes out of it into a colostomy bag which is removable and can be emptied throughout the day. They gave us some leaflets, as well as a fake stoma - a red, circular sponge I could put on my stomach to try to get used to the idea. I put it all in the corner of the dining room and never looked at it. I didn't want to read about it, and I certainly didn't want to talk about it. Heaven help anyone who tried to make me think about it.

And then – blank, nothing for the rest of that day. At some point, I must have called Peter. He said all the right things, more than anyone ever could. I don't remember what they were. I floated around the house, dumbstruck. There was probably television, and internet, and lunch. A nightmare masquerading as a normal day.

In the evening I decided I wanted to curl my hair, for no real reason I could put my finger on other than to create a distraction for myself, or as a feeble attempt to cheer myself up. To make the evening less ordinary in a more ordinary way. There was something optimistic about curling my hair. Dad was at work. Mum was sitting in the lounge, reading or watching television, or doing something else normal. I was going out with my girl friends. We were going to the pub quiz at my local. I wore my favourite asymmetrical blue dress with the sixties-style pattern – red and grey circles, black stripes. The evening was warm and the pub was just two minutes around the corner from my house. It was a beautiful summer's evening, though my stomach was churning too much for me to notice. Everything felt surreal. I was the first of my friends to arrive so I waited outside the door, and my friend Rachael appeared soon after. I briefly told her what Mr Rashed had said and her jaw dropped open as she stared at me in disbelief.

We went inside to wait for the others. They arrived a few minutes later and there was some chatter. Food was ordered. I ate something. The girls talked about something. I listened. I waited for my opportunity to explain why I was so quiet, why I looked so unhappy, because surely I must have. Nobody asked. There just wasn't a good time for me to talk about what had happened. How do you bring up something like that? This thing existed in my head and I needed to let other people know about it too as if that might somehow alleviate the load. It wouldn't – if anything, it would just make it more real. But it's a strange feeling to have a sort of secret that makes you feel so different from everyone else you're hanging out with, who don't have the same huge problem you do.

The girls did the quiz and laughed and chatted and ate – and took photographs to preserve memories of the evening. Of course, who wouldn't want to preserve memories of that particular evening? Three of us smiled for the camera as the fourth stood beside the table, leaning back a little as she tried to fit us all into the frame. The camera captured my curls dropping out as the evening wore on. And an obedient stretching of lips into an upward shape, not reflected in the eyes. Nothing at all in the eyes. Another of the girls stood up and took a photo of the rest of us. In this photograph, I'm slouched forward and my smile is such an obvious lie, it's incredible anyone could be taken in by it.

We all sat back down at the table and continued with the pub quiz. Some of us ordered dessert. Some of us couldn't bear to go through the mundanity of ordering more food, looking at the food, eating the food. Some of us just wanted the evening to be over. One of us just wanted the whole thing to be over. I walked back home not nearly drunk enough, and against my mother's request to ask someone to give me a lift back. I slunk quietly to bed, grabbed a handful of tissues, and bawled. And that was the end of just one of the days I spent trying to be normal.

Sunday was Grandad's funeral. Dad and I drove up together the night before, and Mum rode with Karen and the kids. It was hot and the traffic was terrible for some reason I wasn't really sure of but decided, nonsensically, to blame the World Cup for. It took much longer than usual to get to my grandmother's house. The next day, the church was packed out. We had the wake at the local cricket club. For once, my operation wasn't the big thing at the forefront of my mind, but I only remember snippets of this time. I think there was also pizza, with the cheese on top of the toppings instead of underneath it. I don't know if it's because my main health problems have been sort of related to the digestive system and have at times affected what I have been able to eat, but I always remember the food, whatever the story is. They were strange times, for sure.

Five days later, my mother wanted to show me a text message she had received from my sister. She opened up the messages screen on her phone and selected one, but it wasn't the one she wanted. This one was a message Karen had sent to her ex-husband and then forwarded to Mum so she could talk to her about it. In the message, Karen was telling him that I had cancer. I saw the message briefly before Mum realised it was the wrong one and closed it.

"I don't have that," I said, unable to say the word. "Why would she say I have that? I don't have that."

I can't remember what Mum said, but I remember repeating myself an awful lot before running up to my room, upset. It felt complicated at the time because I'd had the polyps removed, but yes, of course, eventually I realised that I did have that, or at least, I *had* had it.

Years later I would think about my brother and try to slot him into the scenario. I imagined that had he still been alive, he would have happened to come over to the house, Mum would have spoken to him, and he would have come upstairs to see me. He'd talk to me about his own experience with cancer and he would make me feel better. I don't know what he would say, but he would help somehow, because he was my big brother, and that is what I imagined big brothers to do. As he had died of a brain tumour when he was sixteen and I was just one year old, I had never known what our relationship would have been like, and will never know. It is a strange thing for a family member to die when you are a baby. It is a strange thing to have never really grieved for that person, to hear things about them and to have knowledge, but not memories. Facts aren't really the same, and other people's memories are not my own. It has always like it's everyone else's loss and not mine in the same way, like I'm not part of it somehow. So it feels sort of nice to imagine him appearing now, long after he has gone, and thinking about what life might be like if things had been different.

Besides wishing I had known my brother, as far as support networks go mine is pretty great. I was probably quite difficult to deal with at the time this was all happening because talking about it made it scarier, so I would shout at anyone who tried to talk to me about it. Though I may be biased, I don't think I was too bad to live with. I lived with my parents at the time, and we've always been a close family. My dad worked as a train driver and has a strong work ethic. He would do overtime and put up with nightshifts in order to look after us all and give us nice things, like holidays to Florida, my favourite place in the world. He may have seemed a bit scary to my friends when we were kids (and to my boyfriends, which Dad was obviously pleased about), but he always has good intentions and wants to help often, with anything I need. My mother is very gentle and one of the nicest people you'll ever meet, and always tells me her honest opinion about my hair, clothes, other people and all sorts of things – a compliment from her is as invaluable as her kind criticism. I had a wonderful childhood and couldn't have asked for anything more, and I absolutely adore my parents.

And then there's Peter, my rock. We are very silly together and have a lot of fun, and I think we balance each other out quite a lot. I'm impulsive and impatient and keen to do everything immediately even if it isn't the right time or the right way to do it. Peter is more careful with commitments and money and likes to think things through. I like to think I arrange fun things for us to do and bring a little excitement to our lives (like holidays and hot air balloon rides), while his sensibility keeps us grounded when necessary. We complement each other when it comes to looking after our house, too – he deals with keeping things functional and working, and I make the house a cosy home. He is very logical and calm and practical in a crisis, and when I'm upset he can talk me down.

The date for my operation was set for 27th July. About three weeks before, my dad and I went to a pre-op assessment, aptly taking place in what my dad called "the bowels of the hospital" as we had to go down a couple of flights of stairs to get to it. The nurse asked me lots of questions about my health and medical history and talked us through the whole procedure. What was helpful was that she didn't just tell us the medical side of what the surgeon was going to do, but how I should expect to feel after the operation. She empathised with me by saying that a lot of people who have this operation do so because they have something wrong with their bowels that means the operation would give them a better quality of life. She gave the example of another patient whose muscles weren't working properly so when she went to the toilet, she had to get the poo out with her hands. She was happy to be having the operation to solve this horrible sounding problem. Whereas for me, I hadn't really experienced any problems and was probably going to feel worse in comparison. The nurse was very kind and informative, and I left the hospital that day feeling happier than I thought I could have, knowing a little more about what to expect. I was prepared.

There were a few good times still to be had while I was waiting for my operation. They came in the form of nights out with friends – a big group night out from around that time is one of my happiest memories not just of that time, but of all time so far. Nine of us went to a cocktail bar where we had our own private, closed-off seating area with drinks and finger food. Garlic bread, onion rings, breaded mushrooms, dips. And for dessert – rocky roads, chocolate Rice Crispy cakes. But to start us off, some kind of pink drink served in a champagne glass with a strawberry and sugar around the rim. There was music and dancing and laughter – so much laughter. There is a photograph of me laughing my head off at something and it's not a good photo of me at all, but it's great because I look so very happy. That was also the night my friend Emma told me she was planning on moving back to the area after being away at university on the south coast, so it was a very good night.

The final night out before my operation came the very night before I went into hospital. I wanted to do something that night to take my mind off what was about to happen, so Emma, Rachael and I went bowling. Of course, any attempt to take my mind off the thing was futile, really. But when the end of the last game came and we left, I asked the girls to come back to mine and chill for a bit. They agreed and we sat in what my family called the pool room (as in the table, not the swimming) for a while, watching TV. We didn't say very much. I guess we all knew I was trying to hold back the night a bit. I just didn't want to be alone with my thoughts.

I went into hospital the night before my operation, so I had a night alone on a noisy ward to fret about my upcoming surgery some more. A chance to get acclimatised, perhaps. I spent most of that day before the surgery trying not to cry. I was so scared of going to theatre. Looking back, I don't know why I didn't just let it out. There was nothing wrong with showing that I was scared. I suppose I just don't like crying in front of people. One of the women on the ward took pity on me and let me cry on her shoulder that night. Her name was Andre, and she very helpfully tried to reassure me because she'd had the surgery already, during a previous hospital stay. I was worried about getting an enema in the morning because I didn't know what it was going to be like. Which sounds silly now – I was going to have major surgery but I was worried about getting an enema. I guess I was worried about everything because it was all so unfamiliar. Nowadays, I think the more different medical experiences I go through, the more I can tick off the list and they will be more familiar to me if I have to go through them again. A bit of a bleak outlook, but at least I'd know what to expect. A lot of the fear is the not knowing, the unfamiliar situations, the being alone with only other sick strangers for company most of the time. If I tried to pinpoint it, I wouldn't even think I was afraid of things going wrong. I was just afraid. It's a very lonely place to be even if you're surrounded by friends and family because the only one going through your exact experience is you. I wouldn't say I wasn't afraid of death, it's just that the thought of dying wasn't at the forefront of my mind. It was a fear of living afterwards – of being ill, of pain, of a long recovery, of my body.

The next morning they wheeled me down and I lay waiting to go into the anaesthetic room. The nurse who was sitting with me tried to distract me by talking to me about holidays and things like that. It didn't completely work, but it was appreciated. We went into the room and I sat up so that they could put an epidural in my back, which was very painful and even felt a little violent. I laid back and noticed that the anaesthetist was wearing a bandana which had yellow smiley faces wearing stethoscopes on it. I wanted to tell him I liked it but I never did, perhaps not wanting to distract him from what he was doing. But knowing he had a sense of fun made me feel safe and looked after, somehow. It's funny what makes us feel more comfortable in these kinds of situations.

When I woke up from the operation, I was so cold. I had tubes everywhere including up my nose, and I wasn't allowed to drink so my mouth was really dry. A nurse gave me a wet paper towel to put between my lips, but it was really my throat that was the problem so that didn't make much difference. My family came to visit me and I felt like I must have looked terrible – or even a bit ridiculous, being the only one there fitted with tubes and a new colostomy bag.

I spent a week in hospital and most of it was under a misty fog of morphine. I now had a stoma, but I didn't want to look at it so I spent the first few days ignoring it completely. My friends and family came to visit me and I listened to them talking but I wasn't really there. My back ached and there was only one position I could sleep in, and with the noise and the lights and the night-time observations from the nurses, I didn't sleep well. One night I had a half-sleeping, half-awake dream that someone was trying to give me chemotherapy. I heard some sort of trolley trundling down the corridor and thought they were coming for me. There was a man in another ward shouting. They had come for him, and now they were coming for me. I was grateful for the morning light that brought with it the reassurance that my worst fears weren't coming true.

I spent a few days bedridden, except to sit on my chair briefly when my bed needed changing. Getting out of bed was a challenge in itself – the trick was to very carefully roll on my side and put my legs down first. I'd sit tight for a few minutes and then get right back into bed, as it took far too much energy to be upright. Getting back into bed was even more difficult than getting out of it as I had to swing my legs back up while trying not to use my stomach muscles.

And then one day, a woman from the physio department took me for a walk. We only went to the corridor and back, but it was so hard. Especially because she was asking me questions about my tattoo – it was very nice of her, but it was difficult enough to walk, let alone talk at the same time. I held onto her and my IV stand, hunched over and pained. Eventually, I would have my catheter taken out and have to walk to the toilet every time I needed to pee. Having a catheter in after an operation is actually brilliant because it saves you getting up and walking about – though if you do need to get up for any other reason, you have to lug the thing about with you. Other positives after surgery included my sudden taste for chicken soup, which I later blamed the morphine for as I haven't touched it since. And the anti-sickness medication I was on, which was amazing. Obviously, it wasn't good being sick, and every time I did throw up I worried that I was taking a step backwards instead of moving on with my recovery like I needed to. But when I requested anti-sickness medication I was given it through my drip and it made me feel really light-headed, woozy and a bit drunk. Kids, drugs are sometimes good (in moderation, when you need them). I was loving life on that stuff.

By the end of the seven days, when I started to feel better and was no longer being sick, I became bored and desperate to go home. I wanted my own bed and my family. The nurses were almost all wonderful, and while it felt strange at first to be looked after by people I didn't know, I soon got used to it. But I didn't develop a rapport with them in the way that some of the women on the ward seemed to. And all the stories I had heard about people who made friends with other cancer patients, never happened for me. I kept to myself at the best of times, never mind when I was ill – I just didn't have the energy for much conversation.

On my last day when Mr Rashed came to see me on his rounds, he asked how I was and I just told him I wanted to leave. He laughed at me, which I didn't appreciate at the time. But maybe it was because if you want to leave, you're probably feeling quite a bit better. I know that was probably also true because that was the first day in the hospital that I listened to music. Every other day, I was too tired or sick to contemplate doing much apart from staring at the walls, but when I finally played some music, I wondered why I hadn't done that earlier because it reminded me of home, of me. I listened to Alkaline Trio, one of my favourite bands at the time, and I realised how much I missed it. Listening to music really felt like coming home, like being transported away from the hospital. I wished I hadn't waited so long to do it. The boredom of the hospital isn't too bad when you're out of it on drugs or in pain, but it starts to get to you when you've been there for a while and feel ready to leave. Mr Rashed agreed that I could go, and I eagerly got my parents to come and pick me up. For this momentous event, I wore the green slip-on trainers I had with me and a long black skirt with a frilly hem that I usually saved for nights out. I felt ridiculous but I couldn't wear jeans or anything else with a tight waistband because my stomach was too sore. A nurse complimented my shoes, which was very kind of her because I must have looked a sight.

Before I left, one of the stoma nurses showed me how to put on the colostomy bag. It came in two parts – the flange and the bag. The flange was round and sticky with a hole in the middle. I simply had to fit it over the stoma so that it poked through the hole. It had a sort of Tupperware fixture on it and the bag could be clicked into place over the top of it. I listened and watched but I was quite worried that I wouldn't be able to manage it myself, or that I would get it wrong somehow. But the stoma nurse said the stoma had a lovely spout on the top where the waste would come out, so I thought surely it couldn't cause too much of a problem.

Unfortunately, when I got home we discovered that the stoma had other ideas. It didn't want to use its lovely spout and instead, the waste came out at the bottom of the stoma, and it leaked under the flange and onto my skin instead of going into the bag. I didn't know what I had done wrong and panicked that I would never be able to handle looking after this thing. What was to become of me if I couldn't deal with my new body? I laid on my bed with the bag off and my stoma showing its mischievous self proudly to the world, while my mother got on the phone to the stoma nurse. She told us to come back in and she would see me. So just a few hours after I had been released from hospital, we were back in the outpatients department. I had visions of having to stay overnight in hospital again if they couldn't somehow sort it out for me. Thankfully the stoma nurse, Sarah, was very reassuring and found a different colostomy bag that would work better with my stoma. Sarah was an incredibly warm, cheerful and reassuring person, and one of the people from the NHS that I will always remember and be grateful for. All cleaned up and fixed, I could go home and try again. Everything was okay – well, as okay as it could possibly be.

The first few weeks of recovery were very monotonous. I would come downstairs in the morning, sit on the couch and watch television or maybe read a book, and go back up to bed at the end of the day. My back still ached but it wasn't comfortable enough for me to sleep on my side yet. Life was generally painful and uncomfortable.

I slowly built up my stamina with trips to the supermarket, where I would lean on the trolley as my parents went around, or walks around town, where I had to stop for a rest on a bench every few minutes. It was too tiring to walk very far or very fast, or even to stand up for more than a couple of minutes – and when I did I was still hunched over. I lost a stone in weight and despite my pre-op appointment, I was unprepared for just how painful and difficult recovery turned out to be. I don't think you can ever really be fully prepared for it.

A few weeks after my operation, my parents and I saw Sarah at the supermarket. She was very happy to see that I was wearing jeans – a big step after wearing stretchy skirts while I was waiting for my bloated stomach to go down and for my normal clothes to feel comfortable again. Anything that made me feel more normal was very welcome.

My friends took me out while I was recovering. Emma picked me up and took me to see her new flat now that she was living in town again, and when I was more active we also went to a forest to find leaves and acorns for her reception class at her new teaching post. This was several weeks before I could drive again. I was off work for three months in total, while I recuperated and tried to make friends with my new stoma and the world of colostomy bags.

Every couple of days my mum helped me change my colostomy bag. (I emptied it down the toilet when I needed to, but the whole thing only had to be completely removed and replaced every three days or so.) This involved me lying on the spare bed while mum took off the bag and the flange and put new ones on. It was a new and very weird world for us both, and one that seems very alien to me now. While Mum changed the flange, I would cross my fingers that the stoma wouldn't erupt while it was naked. Sometimes it did and the waste would drip out onto my belly, so we tried to do it before I'd eaten breakfast so that my body didn't have anything to work on and spit out, but it didn't always work out. Because my food's journey through my digestive system was now a lot shorter without my large intestine, the stuff that came out was pretty acidic and getting it on my skin stung a lot. This was one of the worst things about managing life with a stoma. The other thing was leakages and spills. I could feel when the bag needed to be emptied – because it had fluid in it, or because I had a lot of gas and the bag had filled up with air like it was about to explode. The output from the stoma varied – it was either really watery, in which case it would sometimes leak, or it would be much thicker. Sometimes it was so thick that it would do something called pancaking. This was when the waste didn't fall down into the bag but instead sat at the top of it and caused a bit of a mess. This happened one day when I went to the gym – possibly the first or second time I went after my surgery. It felt so good to be back there – I felt a sense of contentment and freedom at the gym, knowing I had an hour or two to myself, to do something good for my body, to have a little time alone doing whatever I wanted. I would go during the day when it was quiet, and it was my happy place. I remember walking through reception to the changing rooms and taking in the familiar smell of the gym – the showers, the pool, just some sort of refreshing, new and comforting smell the gym always had. And in that moment I felt like I had come home. Usually, I might go on the treadmill, bike and cross-trainer on the mezzanine level overlooking the first floor of the gym. This part was usually almost empty and it was nice to people-watch while I worked. But this time I wasn't quite ready for proper exercise yet, so the pool would have to do. I had a sort of wide, elasticated, skin-coloured band that I wore around my waist. It went over my colostomy bag to keep everything secure and make me feel more confident while swimming. I had a relaxing swim and a sit in the steam room and the jacuzzi, and successfully showered with my stoma and got changed. Then, to the café for lunch. I liked to have a tuna and cheese panini while I sat by the window watching swimmers go up and down in the pool. However, on that day my lunch was rudely interrupted when I could suddenly feel a wet patch forming on my top. My bag was pancaking. I didn't have any spare colostomy bags with me and I didn't feel confident changing it on my own yet, so I left the rest of my lunch uneaten, picked up my bag and drove straight home, upset that I couldn't just have a nice time doing the things I used to do. I did go back to the gym after that, and things did get better. I like to think that if my colostomy had been permanent, I would have tried harder to look after it myself. But I knew it was only temporary, and I lived at home, and my mum would always help me. I was scared to look after it by myself, though if it had been permanent I would have had to get used to it.

It had taken a while to get to the point where I could even drive to the gym and have a gentle swim. And while I was recovering physically, I was still scared about the future. I didn't know that all this would ever happen to me, and I felt like it left no boundaries for what could possibly happen next. Thankfully at my follow-up appointment with Mr Rashed a few weeks after my operation, he told me I didn't need chemo, and I rejoiced. Finally, a good hospital appointment. I still had further surgery and check-ups to contend with, but at least the thing I was most afraid of wasn't happening.

Three months after my operation, I went back to work at Sainsbury's. I started with two-hour shifts, which were still pretty tiring when I was on my feet — after all, it hadn't really been that long since I'd had major abdominal surgery. Instead of working on the checkout, I was looking after the self-checkout machines or I was on the cigarette kiosk so that I didn't have to lift anything heavy.

One day when I was due to go to work, I woke up to a strange noise. It sounded like someone pushing clothes hangers along a wardrobe rail, so I thought it was my mum putting laundry away in another room. I rolled over and looked around, and saw a bird fly across my bedroom. I jumped up and ran to the door, then turned and looked around. A small brown bird was standing by my wardrobe. I closed the door a little and went downstairs.

"There's a bird in my room."

"What?" Mum said, looking up from her book.

"There's a bird in my bedroom."

"Are you sure?"

"Yes, come and have a look!"

I led her upstairs and showed that indeed, there was a bird in my bedroom.

"I thought you were dreaming!" Mum said. She opened a window and we watched as the bird crashed into the part of the window that doesn't open a couple of times, before finally flying outside. I had no idea how the bird got into my room in the first place, but I wondered if it symbolised something. Like the opposite of a crow appearing in a house to symbolise death. A common brown bird to symbolise everything slowly going back to normal.

Chapter Three
Filling up the Bucket List

I got the phone call on Christmas Eve 2010 to book in my next surgery a few weeks later, and in January 2011, my stoma was reversed. This meant that the surgeon constructed a kind of makeshift large intestine out of part of my small intestine, called an internal pouch (or a J-pouch, which refers to the shape of it, although I don't know what shape mine is). My plumbing would go back to a sort of normal – I'd be pooping out of my butt the same as most people, at least, but things would be a little different on the inside. For this operation, I was only in hospital for three days, but it was still pretty intense. In the days after the operation, I was being sick a lot, partly because of the anaesthetic and partly because my new plumbing hadn't kicked into action yet. One afternoon it was visiting time and the man who was visiting the woman in the bed next to me took the sick bowl off my table, probably thinking it was his wife's, and gave it to her. I watched him with concern, thinking I would probably need the bowl myself fairly soon. And sure enough, a few minutes later when my parents had arrived, I was sick *everywhere*. All over my bed, my nightie and my dressing gown. And it wasn't sick, because I hadn't really been eating much – it was bile. Loads and loads of lovely green bile. I just sat in it and cried. What had I done to my body, agreeing to this surgery, which was really non-essential? I could have carried on with my colostomy and avoided this pain and sickness. Had I made a horrible mistake? I was at a point of complete despair, which I would come to know quite well after future operations, too. It's the low point of feeling so awful physically that I felt like there was no end in sight. My mum helped me to clean myself up and a nurse changed my bed. I was given the anti-sickness medication that felt to strangely good and I was flying again. But I was told that if I didn't start keeping food down soon, I would have to be fed through a tube, which scared me. Fortunately, that didn't happen – my pouch woke up either that same day or the next. This was one of those times when I was very happy to have pooped. A vital rite of passage for getting better and leaving hospital. I stopped being sick and was able to go home soon after.

But now that my pouch was up and running, a big learning curve followed. I had to test foods to see which ones made me go to the toilet more often, and I kept a log of how often I went each day. The first day at home, I went to the toilet seventeen times. The pouch was very active and the output would be very watery or thicker depending on the things I ate. The operation wasn't nearly as bad as the last one, but I had to think about the food I chose for a while, and spicy food was out of the question for a bit. Remember having my colostomy bag changed and the acidic output sometimes stinging my skin? Well, that was now coming out of my butt. I would have the song *Ring of Fire* going around my head while I was sitting on the toilet, which was a new and interesting way for my brain to torture me. It got better and it isn't a problem now, but my superpower is that I can tell the future of Peter's (or anyone else's) bowel movements. That is, if we have a spicy curry I'll feel the effects a couple of hours later, and I'll be able to tell him what will be in store for him the following morning. I do have my uses!

Going to the toilet with the pouch was new territory, and somewhat embarrassing because it seems that when they removed my colon they also removed some sort of muffler that makes pooing a bit quieter. Because I go to the toilet so often with the pouch, I don't fart very often – when I do, it's actually quite amusing and exciting for me, weird as that sounds! But because I go to the toilet a lot, that's when the air usually comes out. And wind is noisy. You know how girls tend to go to the toilet together when they're out and about? Yeah, that's something I try not to do anymore. I don't want people to hear my trumps echoing around the ladies' room. If it's already noisy in the bathroom or I'm just with my mum or on my own, it's fine. Otherwise, hand dryers and toilet flushes are my friends. Wait for the prolonged mechanical whir of the hand dryer and then it's all systems go – let it rip, safe in the knowledge that nobody is going to hear!

I was still glad to be rid of the colostomy and as we packed up the bags and supplies I hadn't used to return them to the hospital, the days of having a stoma felt like they were about twenty years in the past. It was very strange to see it all laid out on the table, as if it belonged to someone else and the last six months had never happened.

I hoped fiercely that 2011 would be a much better year, and it certainly brought some highlights and some changes. In February I drove down to Norwich to go to a Good Charlotte concert with Al, who was at university there. It was about a hundred miles, and I had never driven that far by myself before. I'm not very keen on driving if I don't know where I'm going, so it was a bit of an achievement for me. That was also the month I got my second tattoo – a pink lotus flower on my wrist as a nod to my turn to Buddhism. It was inspired by one of my favourite Buddhist quotes, which felt quite apt at the time:

> *"As a lotus flower is born in water, grows in water and rises out of water to stand above it unsoiled, so I, born in the world, raised in the world having overcome the world, live unsoiled by the world."*

I hoped that I was like a lotus flower, cancer having made me more resilient, or to even not have changed me at all. I wanted to be optimistic and happy despite the horrible experiences I'd endured. I wanted to be that higher being, living above the dirt and still shining.

In March I finally left Sainsbury's and got a job working for a local training company, but it wasn't quite the career take-off I might have imagined my first proper job to be. The company was owned by a couple who offered training in the workplace. Unfortunately, that offer of training did not seem to extend to their new hire, and after two disastrous weeks working for them (in their house, where duties included chasing up sales leads, putting training materials together, creating email newsletters, picking up their medicine prescriptions and feeding the cat), we decided to part ways. I hadn't expected there to be so many sales calls involved, which I hated – especially when either of them was in the room listening to me. I hated talking on the phone, anyway. I've gotten better as it as I've got older, and I'm fine when I know exactly what I need and what I'm going to say. It's not so easy when you're doing a new job you've received hardly any training for, fresh out of your first little part-time job. Luckily most of the people I had to talk to weren't available whenever I called. (Of course, they had good gatekeeper receptionists to keep people like me from talking to the important people.) One morning when I walked in and gave them a cheery hello - to which the wife didn't respond - her more amiable husband asked me how I thought it was going. I admitted it was a bit of a struggle, and he suggested we call it a day. So they sort of fired me, it was sort of mutual. I gave his house key back to him and made sure I got the petrol money they owed me from driving to an event they needed me at the previous week, and just ten minutes after my shift started I was walking back to my car and heading home. I was glad to be out of there but disappointed to find myself suddenly unemployed. I felt like I had failed and let myself and my family down. Admittedly, I did enjoy having so much free time in the three months that followed — working on my poetry magazine and my own creative writing and going to the gym whenever I wanted. The job search became tedious but I kept my chin up – in 2011 my mantra was: "Bowel cancer is a problem; this is not a problem." My theory was that because I had dealt with cancer, nothing else should worry or scare me anymore. A complete fallacy, of course.

I found myself new employment in June, doing administrative work for a mortgage company on a six-month temporary contract. It was an office with three small teams and my job involved data entry, filing, requesting forms, mailing letters, that kind of thing. If doing admin work taught me one thing, it was how easy it is for something to go wrong because of human error – and perhaps badly designed computer systems. The systems we worked with were pretty old fashioned, but they had a messaging feature. So if, for example, a customer called the customer service team to make a payment, the customer service team could send me a message to say that the fee had been paid. This was very useful, except there was no notification system so it was up to me to check for these messages regularly to make sure I didn't miss anything. Part of the job involved sending reminders or warning letters to people who hadn't paid their fees. I had one customer who hadn't paid, so when I realised it was time to send them their final, strongly worded warning letter, I went ahead and printed it off, ready to be mailed out. It wasn't until later in the day after I had done this, that I checked my messages and found a note from customer services saying the customer had paid in full that day. And there I was, about to send an angry letter accusing them of not paying. As my panic rose, I stood up and, trying to look calm, walked out of the office. Once out of sight, I ran downstairs to my friend who was stood at the franking machine with a sack full of letters.

"Emma! Stop! Am I too late?!" I said, running up to her.

"What's the matter?" she asked.

"I have a letter in there that shouldn't go out because the people have already paid and I didn't notice!" Emma stood aside while I rummaged through the bag and retrieved the letter. I had only just prevented myself from getting into trouble and causing a lot of aggravation for a customer, who would have rightly been very annoyed at being harassed about payments for no reason. It made me feel a little more sympathetic towards companies and staff who make simple errors that cause problems for people – it's so easily done.

I enjoyed the job, but while I was sad to be leaving I was also quite relieved because two weeks before my contract ended (on my birthday, in fact), it was announced that the office was shutting down and the department was moving to the company's headquarters about 25 miles away. My last day was the final working day before Christmas, and I left with a goodbye card, a gift voucher, a bath set, and to top it all off, a huge box of Milk Tray I'd won in the tombola. It was a great day to end on, and I was in chocolate heaven.

It was around the time I started that first office job, that I ran my first Race For Life. My girl friends were doing it and I decided that I, too, could train, run, and raise money for Cancer Research UK. It turns out I am not as athletic or as enthusiastic about running as my friends are, but I did raise over £300 for the charity. (A good sob story will get you quite far in that respect.) When we set off running, Emma said she was very proud of me, which was such a lovely thing to hear from a friend and something I would hold on to for a long time. I thought maybe I should be proud of me too, for getting fit enough to run after my surgery and being emotionally resilient enough to want to try. I wasn't very fast, but I would run the race a couple more times in the years that followed, before swearing off it for the sake of my own mental health. Raising money for a cancer charity means thinking quite a lot about the circumstances that led me to do that, and those constant reminders can be upsetting if you're not in the right frame of mind to think about it.

More fun followed in August when I went to Florida for two weeks with my entire family – my parents, my sister, my niece and nephew, my sister's husband, and his three boys. I am always so excited to visit Florida, but this time was even more exciting because so many of us were going. My parents and I stayed in a hotel while my sister and her family rented a villa, where we would visit for dinner and stay over after a drink or two. There is something absolutely magical about Florida – it is actually like being on another planet entirely. Yes, the weather is good and the theme parks are great. But the food is also awesome, the people are all really friendly, the adventure golf is fun and so is the shopping, and everyone is happy. There is nowhere like it that I know of, and nobody is too old for Disney. There is something in the atmosphere that makes the whole place really special – not just Disney, but Universal Studios, International Drive – even remembering standing outside the airport waiting for my dad to pick out our rental car makes me grin. Just thinking about going makes my belly do a little flip, but there is always a long wait ahead of me since we book around a year in advance. The countdown is long but it's worth the wait – and the money, and the long flight. On this particular trip, my mum and my nephew came with me to see Alkaline Trio at House of Blues at Disney Springs, or Downtown Disney as it was known back then – Brandon's first ever gig at fourteen years old. More musical delight.

But it turns out that even with so many other things going on, I'm never far away from the cancer world. In September of that year, I went to an appointment for genetic counselling with my parents. I had been referred because I was so young to have colon cancer that they thought it may have been caused by a genetic defect running in our family. We had blood tests and my biopsy from my operation was tested, and it was confirmed that all three of us had Lynch syndrome. Lynch syndrome is a genetic condition that makes it more likely for a person to get cancer. In other words, it's the world's worst loyalty programme. When we first saw the genetic counsellor she said it could have been something else called familial adenomatous polyposis (FAP), or something else I can't quite remember – whatever it was, Lynch syndrome sounded like the worst of the options, and it turned out to be the conclusion. I try not to think about it too deeply because it scares me. Everyone has genes that work to prevent them from getting cancer, but with Lynch, this gene doesn't work, so your chances of getting the disease are higher. It was explained to us that each person inherits two copies of this particular gene from their parents. So if a parent has one good gene and one faulty gene (and therefore they have Lynch syndrome), you might get the good one or the bad one, and the same with the other parent. My parents each had one good gene and one faulty gene. I received both of their faulty genes. Inheriting one faulty gene means you have Lynch syndrome, but two? I don't know if that makes me doubly likely to get cancer. I try not to think about it because it is terrifying.

The main risk from Lynch syndrome is bowel cancer, and your chances of getting that are 80%. That's huge – so knowing that, I'm not at all surprised that I ended up with it. Exactly which types of cancer Lynch syndrome makes you susceptible to depends on which type of Lynch syndrome you have – mine is PMS2. It is very scary to think that a part of your body that is supposed to protect you doesn't work and that anything could be happening inside your body to harm you and you may not have a clue about it. Thinking about what else could happen makes me panic. Walking into town with my mum one day, I told her I was like a ticking time bomb. "I know," she said.

My sister got checked too and luckily she didn't have it, so she hadn't passed it onto her children. However, we thought that my brother had probably had it. We didn't know for sure but we guessed that his brain tumour was caused by him having Lynch syndrome, too. This is the biggest thing that makes me worry when I think about it. What if my Lynch syndrome causes me to have a brain tumour too?

Back in 1987 when my parents found out about my brother's illness, they tried to figure out what had caused it. The electricity substation just a couple of doors down from my childhood home? Radiation from Chernobyl, the year before? Finally, 22 years later, there was an answer – and I was the vehicle for the message.

With our genetic counsellor at the hospital, we created a plan so that I could have regular check-ups. Every year I would have a check-up on the pouch, which would be a flexible sigmoidoscopy (or flexi sig) – like a colonoscopy but a lot quicker and less invasive. I would also have a gastroscopy to look inside my stomach and small bowel, which is a camera that goes down the throat. I had CT scans for a few years too, and these were definitely the easiest check-ups to deal with. I got – and still do get – so anxious when a check-up comes around. I have an appointment every year with Mr Rashed and he usually plans to send me for check-ups in the coming months. The letters for each appointment will then come in the post, along with an enema I need to give myself for the flexi sig, which feels as undignified as it sounds. I hate the anxiety of receiving a letter that's clearly from the hospital. *Post apocalypse*, you might call it. The appointment might not be for a month or so, and once I've booked the time off work, I'll put it out of my mind quite easily for a couple of weeks. It's a bit of a honeymoon period. Then the appointment will get closer. I'll start to think about it more. *I don't want to go. I hate hospitals. I hate having to go to these things. What are they going to find? Will it all be okay? The procedure is so uncomfortable. What if they find something and I have to go through more tests, more surgery, or the scary unknowns – chemo, radiotherapy?* The anxiety gets worse the closer it gets to the appointment. I'll forget about it during the day because I'll be distracted by something else, but then I'll remember and my stomach will lurch. Not so much with the CT scan because that's just some dye put in through IV, and then a quick ride through a tunnel. And the flexi sig is a piece of cake in comparison to the gastroscopy. That's the only one I insist on sedation for. I open my mouth and the doctor sprays inside it with something sort of banana flavoured, which I swallow and it makes my throat go numb so that they can put the camera down there. It feels like my throat is closing up but I have to remind myself that it's really fine. Then I lie on my side and they give me the sedation, before putting the camera in, which is quite uncomfortable. I hate the camera because it makes me gag. And the whole thing makes me nervous because while you're lying there you can hear them talking, and it's difficult to tell if they have found something or not. The sedation makes me feel sort of drunk and relaxed while it's happening, and then when it's finished I feel groggy and don't remember much about it. Sometimes the consultant tries to tell me what they have found while I am still sedated, which is rather pointless but the nurse goes through it with me again afterwards. For me, sedation is definitely the way to go for a gastroscopy, especially as I did it without sedation once and it was very uncomfortable and made me very nervous.

Sedation isn't offered for a flexi sig, but it isn't really needed as it takes hardly any time at all and it doesn't hurt too much. When I had the colonoscopy back in 2010, I had to drink lots of a drink called Klean-Prep, which is a laxative I needed to take so that the inside of my bowel was clear enough for the doctor to see inside and to move around without causing any damage. The drink is disgusting and makes you spend most of the day on the toilet. It's not just the flavour, but the weird murky texture. For the first few years of having the flexi sig, I needed no prep at all. However, as the pouch got better at solidifying waste and acting more like a large intestine, it was decided that I should have an enema beforehand. Luckily, as we have already covered, I lost my dignity long ago – because there's not much dignified about lying curled up on a towel on the bathroom floor, inserting an enema into your own butt and then pooping out what feels like your entire insides. The enema was something I dreaded doing, but once I had done it the first time, I realised it wasn't so bad and I was happy enough to do it again if I needed to.

The anxiety isn't over when the test is done though, of course. With the gastroscopy and flexi sig, if everything is okay I usually find out there and then. If a sample needs to be sent away for a biopsy test, however, or if I've had a CT scan, I need to wait for the results to come back. Which again, can be sort of forgotten about for the first few days. I don't expect to hear back straight away, so I put it to the back of my mind for a while. But when two weeks have passed and there's still no letter, and I call the consultant's secretary or my GP office to try to chase up the results, that's when the anxiety kicks in again. *Why is it taking so long? When will the results come? What will they say?* Eventually, they would hopefully tell me that everything is fine, or I would receive a letter saying so. And that's how it was from 2011 to 2017.

In January 2012 I started a new job that I loved and would keep hold of for the next year and a half. I was on the web content team for an IT reseller. I had my own sections of the website that I looked after, writing descriptions for the products and making sure that all the information and photos were present and correct. I worked with a small team of lovely people, and it was the happiest I had been in a job so far. Continuing my mission to exercise control over my body, I got my third, Alkaline Trio-inspired tattoo that spring. But all was not completely well inside my brain.

At work, I would find myself drifting off and daydreaming about all the things that had happened before. Just going over things in my head, for no reason.

One day, two girls were walking across the room towards me. It looked to me like one was helping the other. They weren't, they were just walking slowly. But my brain transformed this image into a scenario I recognised: one of them was having physio after a massive operation, just like I had. That was why they were walking so slowly, and why they were holding onto each other. I blinked and looked again and saw that of course, that wasn't what was happening. It was like on TV shows when a character sees something but it isn't real and then it flashes back to reality. They weren't holding onto each other at all. I certainly felt like I was thinking too much about everything. And you know you're having a bad time when half of your thoughts involve trying to suppress the other half of your thoughts. That was the conclusion I came to in 2012.

I contacted my A-Level Psychology teacher to ask him if he did any counselling work and whether I could talk to him because it seemed better than going to a stranger for therapy. He had been my favourite teacher at school and was very approachable. However, although he was qualified he no longer practised. He suggested I ask for counselling through my GP because this would be cheaper than going to someone who had their own private practice, and he gave me some brief advice after I explained what the problem was. I was disappointed. I think what I really wanted from him was some sort of shock or sympathy – some expression of sadness that a student he used to teach had cancer. I wanted someone to express as much shock that I still felt, when it seemed like the people around me had – not forgotten, because that would be unfair. But it definitely felt like I should have moved on as everyone else seemed to, and I hadn't.

I wanted to talk to someone who hadn't heard it all before already, and who I wouldn't feel embarrassed about telling my emotional difficulties. I would consider counselling again on and off for the years that followed, but I wouldn't do anything about it until 2017.

In the meantime, I was determined to have some good experiences. If there was an upside to cancer, it was that it gave me a new outlook on life. I felt more grateful for the things I had, perhaps slightly more capable and less scared of some things (though not as much as I would like), and more impatient about doing the things I wanted to do. In 2012 my friend Kieran and I went to a Professor Green gig at a club in Birmingham. He travelled there all the way from West Sussex where he lived. That night I had my first shot, my first kebab and my first and only try of weed. We went up to the car park on the roof of the hotel we were staying in and lit up as we watched drunk people below spill out of nightclubs and have fights outside the kebab shop. I had never even smoked a cigarette before and wasn't really sure how to at first. I'm still not sure if I did it right, which I know is ridiculous. I liked the smell and the taste, but my lungs were very unimpressed, and I didn't like the feeling of intentionally doing something that wasn't right for my body. It made me cough a lot and I wondered why I was inflicting that upon myself. I was happy to have tried it but wouldn't bother again. Instead, it was time to do something else involving a little smoke: in 2013, I decided I wanted to do a firewalk, so I went online looking for one.

It took me a while, but eventually, I found an event that looked great. It was in November and being put on by sight loss charity My Sight Nottinghamshire.

It was to take place around Bonfire Night at Nottingham Castle, and as well as the firewalk there would be fireworks and food stalls. It sounded great. I signed myself up and asked my parents to go with me to watch – though my mum was more than a little reluctant to watch me walk over hot coals. We booked a hotel in the city, and we were good to go.

Unfortunately, that particular night was very windy and most of the event had been called off – there were no fireworks and no stalls. We would still be doing our walk, but not with a colourful backdrop lighting up the castle. There were maybe twenty people taking part in the event, but before we could march over the flames we had to do some training. While there was some safety chat involved, it was mostly motivational stuff to show us that whether or not we could carry out the task depended on whether we had the mental strength and determination to do so. It was interesting to learn about how the body takes its cues from the mind and the things we tell ourselves we're capable of. For example, one of the activities involved partnering up and repeating positive statements about ourselves – "I'm strong, I'm powerful", and so on. We would then bend our arm and raise our fist, and our partner would try to knock down our arm. When we had said those words, we found that our arm stayed firmly upright. However, when we repeated phrases such as "I'm weak, I'm worthless", our arms lost their strength and fell down easily. We had to tell ourselves positive things and give ourselves confidence before doing the firewalk – or anything else we wanted to achieve in life, really. Geared up and ready to go, we made our way outside where our families and friends were waiting for us.

The fire had been lit and was blazing a good couple of feet above the ground, but it would settle down by the time we were ready to start. We took off our shoes and socks, and having fairly sensitive feet, I winced at the feel of the gravel beneath my soles before I was anywhere near the coals.

We lined up and as each of us approached the walk, the trainer would shout "What's your name?" – to make sure we were still in our right minds or something.

When my turn came I shouted my name, and he yelled: "Are you ready?"

"Yes!" I yelled back.

"Go!"

And off I went. Quickly.

That's the knack to it, you see. There's no special footwear, no trickery. The fire is real, and my bare feet speed-walking over them certainly felt it. You just have to keep moving so that your feet aren't touching each coal long enough for it to hurt. My feet were black by the end, and I got a blister despite the whole thing taking seconds. But as I stood next to the woman who had gone before me and we cheered on everyone else as they finished, I felt a great sense of achievement. What a weird and exciting thing I'd just done! I dusted myself off as best I could so that I could put my shoes on and walk back to the hotel, where I washed my feet and we finished off the night with a drink in the bar. I felt accomplished and completely relaxed at the same time. Not only was I happy with what I had done, but I just love staying in hotels and being in a city at night. It was a great combination.

In November 2012 my parents and I moved house. We had stayed in my childhood home until I finished school at the age of 18, and in 2006 we had moved into a gorgeous new house. It was much bigger than my childhood home, which had a living room and kitchen-diner downstairs, three bedrooms and one bathroom. This new house had a big kitchen separate from the dining room, and what had once been a double garage was converted on one side into another room – this would be where the new pool table would go. There was a downstairs toilet, a family bathroom and an en suite, four bedrooms and a conservatory. I adored this house, and I now keep an alert on Rightmove so that I can find out if it ever goes back on the market. But in 2012, we moved out of it. My dad was retiring and with the new house, my parents wouldn't have a mortgage anymore. I was sad to be leaving the house, and not only because I liked it so much. I remembered going for a walk on one of the first days after we moved in, and when I came back and approached the house, I said to myself *I can't believe that we live here. Just look at it.* But the house was also full of memories. It was the house we moved into during the summer between me leaving school and starting university. And I loved university. I met Peter there, as well as other friends, and I was finally done with the guy who I'd been letting mess me around throughout my last year of school. Peter and I had many significant moments in that house. This was the house where I had found out I got into university, and eventually passed my degree, and where my first car was delivered. It was where my niece and nephew came trick or treating at Halloween. It was a house of new beginnings and fun.

But it was also the house where I had cancer, where I worried about going to the toilet for months, where Mum and I dealt with my stoma. The memories weren't all good. I wondered if by leaving the house I might be leaving some of that behind – the illness, the bad thoughts about it, or both. But as I would find out, it doesn't really work like that.

Chapter Four
From Hot Air Balloons To Hot Water

Continuing my penchant for doing new things, in 2013 my family and I were back in Florida because of another activity on my bucket list. I wanted to go to New York. My dad didn't seem too bothered about going, so I said to my mum, "If I pay for us to go to New York together, will you go with me?" And she said yes.

However, I inherited my mother's terrible sense of direction and we couldn't really be trusted to go out so far into the world by ourselves without getting horribly lost. So my dad decided he would come with us after all, but that an eight-hour flight was a long way to go for just a few days. So he said we should go somewhere else while we were there. That's how we ended up going to Florida for nine days, and then New York for six days on the way back. We stayed near Times Square, went up the Empire State Building, saw the Statue of Liberty, walked along the Brooklyn Bridge, and visited The Museum of Jewish Heritage. Tick, tick, tick – that was the sound of my bucket list. I enjoyed New York but Times Square was so horribly crowded, it was a bit of a culture shock for someone living in a much quieter town in Northamptonshire. I did love being in a city I'd seen on so many TV shows and movies, and for a while afterwards, I got excited any time I saw New York on TV, keenly trying to spot a landmark I could recognise from being there in person.

In even more exciting news back home, Peter had bought a flat. I hadn't been in a position to move into it when he was buying it because I was made redundant from the job I had loved so much in the summer of 2013. It was another three months of unemployment before I got a new job at a digital marketing agency. This time I'd be writing adverts, website copy, social media posts and email newsletters for clients such as car breakers yards, dress shops and care homes. It was enough to fulfil my desire to have writing as part of my full-time job. And now that I had some income, I gradually spent more time at Peter's flat and less time at my parents' house. After six months, when I'd had my fill of lugging a bag of clothes from town to town every few days, I moved in properly.

Fast forward another year or so and, settled into my new job and home, I was once again wondering what I could do next. A hot air balloon ride had been on my bucket list for a while, so in 2015 I booked myself and Peter onto one. I was looking forward to it but I was also nervous – I had booked it in excitement when I was drunk at home one evening (whisky and writing were often a standard Friday night) but as the event drew closer I wondered if it was such a good idea. I had to call the company on the day of the flight to make sure it was still happening, as they are sometimes cancelled due to poor weather conditions – not enough wind, too much wind, and so on. As I called them to listen to the pre-recorded message, I half hoped that it would be cancelled. But it was still on, so that evening we drove to the meeting place in the countryside and met up with the pilot (also called Peter) and the other participants. First, some of us had to help get the balloon up and running.

My Peter was among the helpers, holding part of the balloon open so that the fans could blow air into it. When the hard work was done, we climbed into the basket and there was no going back – we were heading up.

And what a beautiful up it was. Flying in the hot air balloon felt very much like floating – I barely felt it lift off the ground. We sailed on the wind over fields and farms and country houses, scaring off sheep that saw our fire-propelled vessel above them and raced away in their herd. We saw big houses with outdoor swimming pools and a gathering of people having some sort of outdoor party with a marquee. We were very lucky that our flight hadn't been cancelled, as many people don't get those perfect weather conditions on the first date they try. It was absolutely wonderful.

When we landed with a bump in someone's field, the experience wasn't over. We had to stamp on the deflated balloon and gather it up to get it back onto the chase truck that had followed us on the ground. Then we hopped on the truck, all eight or so of us stood on the outside of the truck rather than actually in it, as it drove through the field and out onto a nearby road. We stepped off and gathered around for a champagne toast, collected our certificates of achievement, and got taxis back to where we had left our cars. We had started at around six and got home for about 11pm. It was an unexpectedly long but exciting evening.

That year, I was also in the audience for a television show for the first time. Peter and I went to see The Last Leg being filmed live – a Channel 4 chat show about the week's news, with Adam Hills, Josh Widdicombe, Alex Brooker and a couple of different guests on each episode. We got the train down to London and sat in the audience, happily out of view of the cameras for the most part – we wanted to see the show but were happy enough to not be seen on TV. The Last Leg was originally broadcast during the 2012 Summer Paralympics. Adam Hills was born without a right foot and Alex Brooker was born with hand and arm deformities and a twisted right leg, which was amputated when he was a baby, so there are often references to disability in the programme. The show made me laugh, but it also made me think. I loved that the presenters could joke about their missing legs and be comfortable with their bodies, and I wanted to be like that, too. I was already a little like that anyway, but I was surprised how much I could relate to them despite our situations and bodies being quite different. We all had something missing, and the message was that it was okay to be different like that. I felt empowered and like it was okay to talk about my body, when I would often shy away from mentioning it for fear of making other people feel uncomfortable. Cancer is classed as a disability under the Equality Act of 2010, but I don't consider myself to be disabled. I don't feel like that's a category I fit into neatly. And since cancer itself has never made me feel ill or in much pain (it was the surgeries to get rid of it that did that), I don't feel like I fit into the chronic illness category, either. In fact, for a long time, because I'd had surgery and not chemo, I felt like I had never been a proper cancer patient, either. I know better now. I've had enough surgery to no longer be an apologetic patient whose cancer was never bad enough to truly complain about. Surgery is no walk in the park. I think a lot of the time people want to fit in with something, to feel part of a group and be able to define their experiences in that way, and sometimes it isn't so easy to do that because nothing feels like the perfect fit. But The Last Leg did that for me a little, despite my feelings of being in such a different situation.

Over the years after my bowel surgery, I would add more places to the list of countries I had been to. A two-night cruise with work took us to Bruges, Belgium, and Peter and I went to Porto Santo, a small island off Madeira, that same year. We would later visit Fuerteventura in the Canaries, and my parents and I would see Amsterdam, Gothenburg and Stockholm. I don't particularly like travelling – it takes a long time and it's such a lot of hassle – but I love holidays when I get there. Gothenburg and Stockholm fulfilled my need to go to Sweden and absorb the language. I had started to watch a video game YouTuber, PewDiePie, who is Swedish and sometimes spoke the language in his videos – mostly swearing when something scared him in a horror game, so I learnt the naughty words first by accident. But it's a beautiful language and since I had never gotten very far with my attempts at French and Spanish at school, it was good to have a language I could speak a little better. I added learning to speak Swedish fluently to my bucket list, but to this day I'm still working (or forgetting to work) on that one.

I'd also go on to see Slipknot in concert twice (once supported by Korn), as well as Enter Shikari, The Who, and Bring Me The Horizon – a band whose songs about drug addiction ran strangely parallel to my feeling of drowning in fear and past memories. Because despite doing all of these great things, I was still plagued by anxiety and bad memories from everything that had happened to me. I was sort of torn between two ideas – the notion that cancer had made me more impulsive and adventurous, and the feeling that it had given me what at times seemed like post-traumatic stress. I even researched online to see if it was likely that I had PTSD. The truth, I realised later, was that I almost wanted to have PTSD. I wanted an explanation for feeling this way that wasn't simply "it's normal because you had cancer". I would have rather explained away my feelings by giving them a label and blaming it on my mental health. That, to me, was better than thinking that my feelings were completely justified because of my medical history and the threat Lynch syndrome brings with it. It was scarier to think that I was right to worry that the cancer might come back. My symptoms weren't severe enough to be full-blown PTSD, although I definitely experienced anxiety and grief because of the trauma of cancer. I wanted to focus on my mental health and the things that had happened before, not the very real and terrifying possibility of my physical health problems returning.

The stress of it all also manifested physically. In 2014 I began getting headaches. Not severe ones – they were mild, but they stuck around for days at a time so they were a nuisance, and very worrying considering my Lynch syndrome and my brother's death. "Brain tumour" has always been a scary phrase for me (I know it probably is for everyone, but it likely feels like more of a real threat to me than most) and the possibility of me ever having one doesn't bear thinking about. Even saying the words sounds like tempting fate, and I don't even believe in fate. Anyway, you have a headache that won't go away and you start to wonder. And worry. Not enough to go to the doctor yet, and luckily I didn't have to. I booked myself in for a back massage and it did the trick – I had been holding all of my tension in my neck and shoulders, and whether that was causing my headaches or not, I stopped having them after that. I started going for a massage regularly from that point on. Not simply because I want to get rid of back pain, but because I never want to feel worried that there might be something seriously wrong with me when this particular ailment could so easily be fixed. I didn't want that kind of anxiety if I could avoid it.

Around 2014 or 2015 I was invited to go to London to talk to a doctor about getting regular check-ups for uterine cancer and ovarian cancer. This is something I had talked about with my geneticist, but when we'd had the conversation I wasn't quite of an age at which they would normally suggest testing for these types of cancer – hence the wait. We were referred to the doctor in London because there they could do several tests all in one day, rather than having to go to a more local hospital on separate occasions for each scan or test. Peter and I took the day off work and got the train down to London, then the tube across to St Bartholomew's Hospital. It was a hot summer's day and we weren't familiar with that particular area of London, and I was already cranky and anxious. So it didn't help when after a while of sitting in the waiting room, we were told that the doctor had been held up at another hospital and wasn't on site yet and that perhaps we should go away and come back in a couple of hours. So off we went to find a pub to sit in for a while, and we came back later. We waited around for a while longer – so long that I began to worry I had been forgotten about completely – and then I was finally called in to see the doctor. Only to be told that I was a bit young to be having these tests yet, and I should come back when I was 28, a couple of years later. It was the briefest of conversations and felt like a totally wasted trip full of pointless effort and upset. We left and went to get some food, then caught a very busy train home. Tired and annoyed, I called the day a write-off. I never did go back to see him, or anyone else for that matter, about testing for uterine or ovarian cancer, though I did sometimes think about it. I was scared and was already undergoing surveillance for bowel cancer. I didn't want more appointments making me anxious. I would look back on this decision later and consider myself silly, and lucky under the circumstances.

I had a scare in 2016 when I went for my second smear test. Women are invited to smear tests from the age of 25 onwards, every three years. It's not much fun — take off your jeans and undies, spread your legs, and let a nurse hold your vagina open with a metal thing, before rummaging inside it with a cotton swab. The smear test was as painful as it sounds (even though what I read on the internet and in the leaflet said it would just be "uncomfortable" — it was more than uncomfortable for me), and the results came back saying I had abnormal cells and HPV. HPV means there's a chance that the abnormal cells will turn cancerous. Panic. Is it happening all over again?

I had to go for a colposcopy at the hospital, which is like a smear test but they take a biopsy so that it can be tested. A few weeks later I received a letter to say that the biopsy came back with moderate abnormal cell changes and I would have to go back to the hospital to have LLETZ treatment. This is how they get rid of the abnormal cells — more leg spreading and painful rummaging. Of course, this meant tons more anxiety, scary letters in the post, waiting and worrying, Googling and gulping. But after the LLETZ treatment, I received a letter to say that all of the abnormal cells had been successfully removed. I had to go back to my GP for another smear test six months later, and this confirmed that everything was still okay. I was relieved, of course – it had been a scary time and I was dreading the news that there might be something else terribly wrong with me. Even without Lynch syndrome or even any cancer history, this kind of thing would make me worry, as it would anyone, I'm sure. Knowing about my genetic condition and having gone through a cancer diagnosis before made it feel all the more likely that it was happening again. Thank goodness that this time it wasn't.

Going back once more to wanting to get things done, another thing I decided I wanted to do and was therefore going to do, was get a Master's degree. This decision was a little less impulsive than the firewalk and the hot air balloon ride, but once I get something in my head, I don't let go of it easily and it's highly likely to happen, even if it takes a while to figure out how I'll go about achieving it. I eventually chose an online distance learning course that I could do for two years part-time while I worked full-time. It was a lot of money to pay so I had to decide that I was really committed, and I finally settled on MA Creative Writing at Teesside University. Being on the course involved watching videos from the tutors, discussing literature in the course forum and completing assignments. I managed to fit it all in during evenings, my lunch break at work, and weekends. I would go to the gym and read journals while on the exercise bike. After a lot of hard work, I passed with Distinction in October 2017.

It was in October 2017 that my Uncle Mick died of skin cancer. It was 16th October and I remember the day because that was the day the sky turned yellow. Dust from the Sahara was brought to the UK by Hurricane Ophelia, and in the afternoon it made the sky in my part of the world an unusual yellow colour. The sun even looked red in some places. My dad called me that evening to tell me Mick had gone, and I wondered if he had gotten to see the sky's great spectacle before he went. I had gone up to Manchester to see him with my parents a couple of months before he passed away. I hadn't seen him in a long time due to his separation from my aunty, and due to not going up to Manchester to see any family for a few years. The truth is I had been in two minds about whether or not I should go to see Mick. I thought it would be upsetting for me because it would make me think about my own health and whether cancer would come back and kill me someday. Just writing that sounds rather selfish to me now, but when something makes you feel very vulnerable these decisions aren't as easy as they might seem. I am glad I eventually decided to go, with a little prodding from my friend Chris. Chris worked for the same marketing agency as I did until 2017, and I consider him to be my best friend and something of a brotherly figure. We meet up a couple of times a week, and it was during a few of these meetings at a pub in his town, along with his girlfriend Mary, that we talked about Uncle Mick and he encouraged me to go to see him. So my parents and I drove up, and Mick was happy to see us. We helped my aunty and cousins to move his belongings from his flat to my aunty's flat across the road, where he had been staying. It felt good to be a part of helping out, to be a little useful in a practical way.

The last contact I had with Mick was him congratulating me on Facebook for passing my Master's. It was a nice final thing to have. I also love the photographs I have of him picking me up and playing with me at my sister's first wedding. I was seven years old and very light – a bit of a stick with a mop of brown curls on top, really. My uncle and my cousin Peter were always picking me up and swinging me around. I have good childhood memories of them both.

Really, what I was doing when I was umming and ahhing about going to see Mick was a kind of self-preservation. I was trying to teach myself a little self-care by avoiding triggers that would make me feel upset or have flashbacks from my own illness. Whenever I was in a group and someone started talking about someone else who had cancer – whether that was someone they knew or someone famous – I immediately felt defensive and upset. I just didn't want to know, and I tried to shelter myself from the subject as much as I could. After all, I had experienced it and still had to go for regular check-ups. Why subject myself to even more of it if I didn't have to? It was similar to how I was learning when to stop reading things on the internet. I found a few good blogs, forums and Twitter accounts where I could read about other people's cancer experiences, and know that I wasn't alone in how I was feeling. But reading too much, or reading the wrong thing, is the opposite of helpful and

I was slowly learning to tell myself to stop when what I was reading made me feel anxious.

That's also why I only did Race For Life three times before swearing off it. Applying for it, training for it and raising money for it all involved thinking about my own experiences regularly, and it started to feel like too much. In a way, it also felt like it was turning my private experience into a group activity when the people around me couldn't directly relate to having cancer themselves. It made me feel more alone, through nobody's fault - simply because we were there for different reasons.

In the few years after my bowel surgery, it wasn't even that I felt worried about my health or anxious about scans most of the time. It was that I was simply thinking about what had happened. Replaying scenes of being in the hospital or going to appointments, or having flashbacks of these things. It is difficult to explain because when I thought of these things – and when I still think of them – I just feel sad. Maybe it's a little like grief. It feels weird being sad about it because it seems like every feeling has to have a reason - you're unhappy because you're worried about the cancer coming back, or because you're still feeling the physical effects of it from the first time around. But you can just be sad simply because of the fact that it happened, and I'm only just learning that. I'm grieving for a former self – my body before it changed, before it became scarred, before my belly became a bit lopsided through surgery. Back when my body could be trusted. Grieving for the version of me who didn't know of the effects of cancer, who had never had any serious medical problems. A more carefree me.

I think that grief is very real, and maybe it never goes away.

It may even be partly due to that grief that I felt a disconnect between myself and my body. It wasn't until maybe 2017 that I realised I was making things worse by thinking of myself and my body as two separate entities. I had framed my body as the enemy. It had gotten cancer and it had hurt me badly. It had betrayed me, and it might do so again. It couldn't be trusted. I would go to the gym and tell myself I should wear out my body by going hard on the treadmill because that's what it deserved. It should be punished. I was grieving for the body I knew and loved and had lost, and it had been replaced by this strange new one that I didn't like. It took me a long time to identify that this was my way of thinking, to realise that it was unhealthy, and to actively try to modify my thoughts and stop telling myself these things. My body is me – we are in this together. It couldn't help getting cancer, which is the real enemy. I had to try to learn to love my body again and use positive reinforcements to remind myself of all the things I liked about it. I wrote down everything I like about my body – my hands, my boobs, my butt, my legs, my hair. Pretty much everything except the abdomen area, really. Yes, I still thought of my body as a wreckage at times, and I still felt broken, but it helped to stop berating my body as if it were the devil. I wonder if that is a sort of defence mechanism, to try to separate myself from my body so that I blame my body as a separate entity without blaming myself for getting cancer. Or to try to mentally separate myself so that it feels like my body got cancer, not me, and if it happened again, it would be happening to my body and not to me – or to try to prevent it from becoming my identity or taking over in some way.

I finally went to counselling in late 2017. I hadn't been sure if I needed to go, but since I had been thinking about it for seven years I figured there were some things I should talk about. I signed up for six sessions with a local private counsellor, but I didn't really know exactly what I wanted to get out of it or what to expect, and I perhaps needed a little more guidance than I received. I felt very self-conscious and like I shouldn't really be there. It was good to be able to talk about cancer, as well as some other long-standing issues I would have liked to change, such as feeling socially awkward and shy. I wanted to be the person I had been when I was a teenager, or just before my diagnosis, but I couldn't pinpoint exactly what that was like or how to get there. I was essentially the same person but I didn't feel like I was. I felt aged and broken by the disease. At the end of the six sessions, I decided not to go for any more. I wasn't sure if it was really helping, and I felt strange paying someone to listen to me talk. I didn't go there looking for a diagnosis. I knew I didn't really have PTSD, I suppose, though maybe I had some symptoms of it. Going to counselling in a way made me feel like a bit of an imposter or an attention seeker, looking for help when I didn't need it. If I didn't have a diagnosed mental health condition, what was I moaning about? Was my experience really that bad? I had to keep reminding myself that just because you haven't been diagnosed with a mental health problem, doesn't mean that it isn't still a problem or that your anxiety, fear and stress isn't valid. It is still important and worth talking about, exploring, and trying to improve where you can.

I didn't really know what I wanted to get out of counselling. I already had an outlet for my anxiety because I was a writer, and I had been writing about cancer for years at that point. One of the first things I wrote about cancer was a short non-fiction piece called "2010", which was published in the literary magazine Barefoot Review in 2012. I had since been writing poetry about my feelings on cancer, getting them published in literary magazines or posting them on my own website. If I felt the particular need to wallow I would pour myself a glass of Jack Daniels and Coke, put some music on and spend the night writing. Possibly crying. Or maybe just enjoying being creative. The poetry isn't all doom and gloom, but I had a lot to say about what had happened, and poetry was the place for it.

2017 had actually been a pretty bad year, health-wise. I had a recurring abscess down below, which I discovered while in the toilet at work one day. When I first felt it as I was wiping, my stomach flipped and as it was a lump, the C-word was the first thing that came into my head. At that moment, I felt a strange intertwining of both panic and disbelief, both at the same time. I had a look on the internet as soon as I could and after that, and after obsessively feeling it every time I went to the toilet, I was fairly sure it was an abscess. Nothing serious then, but the bad news was that it stuck around for months. Sometimes it would simply come and go without hurting or getting very big at all, but once or twice got so big I could barely sit down in comfort. I was on and off antibiotics all year, which made me worried – I don't like taking too much medication, and I was hearing on the news that taking antibiotics for the wrong things could make them ineffective when you really needed them. Plus, some types of antibiotics had rather unpleasant side effects. One sort I tried just made me hungry, which was annoying because I had to take them on an empty stomach and couldn't eat for an hour after taking them. At one point I was prescribed a different type of antibiotic to see if it helped keep to abscess away, and they made me feel terrible. I went to bed one night feeling like I couldn't quite breathe properly, but I hoped that I would just fall asleep. I sometimes have trouble catching my breath anyway – it was something that happened occasionally and I'd had for years. I put it down to stress or something and didn't really worry about it. But this time I lay awake and my heart started beating really hard. I eventually woke Peter up, convinced he would have to take me to the emergency room because there was something wrong. But as soon as he started talking to me and held me I calmed down. We were fairly sure I was having a panic attack. I blamed the antibiotics and came off them straight away, but it may have been the stress of the whole situation.

After the fifth or sixth recurrence of the abscess, my GP referred me to a general surgery consultant at the hospital. I made the appointment, took time off work and went to the hospital by myself to see this new doctor. The routine of waiting for a letter, getting time off work, waiting anxiously for the date, driving over there, sitting in a boring waiting room full of strangers feeling even more anxious, seeing someone, and then having to make up whatever time I had missed at work. Tedious. The consultant examined it but couldn't see anything as I was on antibiotics and it was already going away. It was quite small at this point. He told me that the next time I got one I should go to A&E so that they could drain it for me and get rid of it for good. So one night when it had reappeared I called 111, explained what the doctor had said, and they agreed I should go to the hospital. Peter and I wolfed down some dinner and then he drove me over there. I felt silly showing up with such a seemingly small problem when other people at the hospital would have far more urgent ailments, but that was what I had been told to do. A&E was busy when we got there, and we were told to go to the urgent care building, which was empty but still involved more waiting. When a doctor appeared and called me into her office, she had a look but said she couldn't do anything with it. She quite bluntly said I'd need a "rather unpleasant" operation to get rid of it for good, which worried me and almost made me scoff at the same time – I'd had my bowel removed, how much worse could an abscess removal be? She gave me a prescription for more antibiotics and I left feeling like she thought I was just an annoying timewaster. We drove back home late and night, and me tearful, so upset that this seemingly small but hugely annoying thing was happening to me after everything I'd already been through.

I took the course of antibiotics but the abscess came straight back, so I called my GP again, who referred me to a consultant at the hospital, again. I was going around in circles and getting quite worried that nobody would be able to sort out my problem. I was lost in the medical system. I couldn't just keep taking antibiotics forever, but an abscess is an infection, so what if I ended up with sepsis if it remained untreated? I felt worried and trapped.

The second consultant sent me for an MRI. More anxiety, but at least I had been for an MRI before and knew the drill. Strangely, the MRI didn't pick up anything around the area of my abscess, but it did pick up something in my womb that needed to be checked out, so I was referred to Mr Doshi, a gynaecologist. Filling defects, the letter said. I had no idea what that meant, and searching on Google (or rather, Peter searching on Google to protect me from any worrying or inaccurate information) brought up nothing of any use. But the abscess was still a problem too, and I wondered if the two things were connected somehow. After all, that was the reason why I had been sent for an MRI.

My worries about the abscess formed part of my conversations with my counsellor, and when we parted she asked me to get in touch in a little while and update her on my medical situation. I never did email her to tell her that everything was okay. Because it wasn't.

Chapter Five
Diagnosis; Burger

My visit to Mr Doshi was very reassuring. Well, it was very stressful because we had to go to a different medical centre I had never been to before, and he was someone I hadn't seen before, but Peter and I went together. Mr Doshi gave me an exam which seemed fine, and he looked at my MRI results. He said he didn't think it was anything to worry about, but I could get a hysteroscopy just to be sure, if I wanted more leg spreading and painful rummaging. I said no because I didn't want to put myself through anything else if it wasn't necessary, and I went away happy.

However, a few weeks later I received a letter in which Mr Doshi basically said that he had changed his mind. I had told him about my Lynch syndrome during the appointment, and he didn't really know anything about it – which was surprising as uterine and ovarian cancer are risks with Lynch syndrome. But in the letter, he said that he had been researching the condition and he thought I should get a proper exam just to be on the safe side, so he was referring me to someone else at the hospital for a hysteroscopy. I had known about the risk of uterine cancer, but like an idiot, I hadn't mentioned it and I hadn't said yes to the hysteroscopy. I was scared of what it might find, and it was much easier to assume that everything was fine. Thank goodness for Mr Doshi, because if I was left to my own devices I could well be dead.

I went for the hysteroscopy and awaited the results. I told them that I was going on holiday soon, so if I needed a follow-up appointment it would have to wait until I got back. Meanwhile, I had also been awaiting my annual appointments that Mr Rashed usually arranged for me. They came much later this time – around March or April 2018, and the more I waited for them the more I worried. I had to do a lot of chasing and ringing around asking what had happened to my check-ups, and that alone was making me nervous. It was also frustrating because it used to be that the hospital could do my flexi sig and gastroscopy at the same time. Well, not exactly the same time – that would be very strange and painful. But flexi sig first and gastroscopy after, with no need to even get up or switch doctors, that was usually the routine. Now the hospital was saying that the same doctor couldn't do both procedures, so I had to make two separate appointments for them. That was, wait for two appointments to come through, and wait anxiously for one date, and then the other appointment days or weeks later. Book time off work twice, go to the hospital twice, wait to be called onto the ward twice, put on a gown and wait in the ward until it's my turn, twice. Have a camera inserted into one hole or another, twice. Be told the results twice. Make up time at work twice. Fear, anxiety, worry. Twice.

It turned out that the flexi sig was fine, but the gastroscopy revealed a polyp which was sent for biopsy. It was flat and to be treated as urgent. That spring was a very stressful time, but I hoped that once all the tests came back everything would be okay. I was glad that it was over for now, and I was looking forward to going away. My parents and I had been planning another trip to Florida, and I had been worried – for months, in fact – that something would come up to scupper our plans. We had visited again for three weeks in 2016 to celebrate my mum's retirement. We had even flown premium and we intended to do the same again this time. Nothing came up between the tests and the day we were due to fly, so in May we went off for our two weeks in the sun. Little did I know I had brought two cancer stowaways with me.

Despite telling the receptionist at the hysteroscopy appointment that I would be away for the first two weeks of May, when I arrived home there was an appointment letter waiting for me – and the appointment was for that very day, just a couple of hours later. We had just arrived back from an overnight flight and then driven back home from Birmingham, and I can rarely sleep on a plane, at least not for longer than a few minutes. So I wasn't really in any state to drive myself to the next town for a surprise hospital appointment. Jetlagged and harried, I got on the phone to explain the situation and rearrange the appointment. Two phone calls later and I had postponed the appointment to the following Friday. I was worried but I relaxed a little knowing that whatever it was surely wasn't that urgent, because apparently, it could wait seven days.

But that wasn't the only nasty surprise coming my way. On Tuesday morning I was back at work when I got a phone call from Mr Rashed's secretary. Mr Rashed wanted to see me on Thursday, and not at his usual outpatient clinic – I had to go and find him on a ward. This was not a good sign. This was something urgent. The biopsy must have come back and shown cancer. I was sure of it. I hung up the phone, went back into the office and asked Nicola, one of the managers, if I could speak to her in the meeting room next door. I tried to look calm and normal but I was panicking inside. I told her about the phone call and said I was scared that it was cancer again, and I did something I'd never done at work before – I cried. She gave me a hug and asked me if I wanted to go home. I said no, that I would be fine. Tuesday was my night to head over to Chris's town and go to the pub with him and Mary, so I didn't really want to go home – at least forty minutes in the other direction – to an empty house instead. I was also supposed to be having lunch with my parents that day, which was another Tuesday tradition. I texted my mum and told her that I had a meeting and that I couldn't go to lunch. I just couldn't face talking to them about it, and they would know immediately that something was wrong even if I tried to hide it. I went back to my desk and tried to work, but of course, I couldn't concentrate. I messaged Chris instead. He had a job interview to go to in the afternoon, but he said I could come to his house if I wanted to.

"If I come over could I stay there while you're out?"

"Of course."

"I will talk to Nicola, maybe go to Tesco and grab some lunch, and come over."

It seemed like a silly reason to go home. I wasn't ill (well, I didn't feel like I was, anyway), and I didn't want to take advantage. But my stomach felt like it was tied in knots and I couldn't sit and work with all the worries in my head while all around me everyone was carrying on as normal. Nicola was happy for me to go home, so, feeling a bit like I was skiving off, I shut down my computer, packed up my bag and headed to Tesco. Sausage roll, Monster Munch and Vanilla Coke all secured, I nipped down the dual carriageway to Chris's house. We sat in his living room where some sort of relaxing music was playing, and we talked about my worries and his impending job interview. My phone rang while I was there and it was the hospital, asking to arrange an appointment for me to have some sort of test. I didn't know anything about it so I told them I wasn't going to arrange an appointment until I had spoken to Mr Rashed and knew what was going on. It was all quite alarming and confusing. Sometimes hospitals are so efficient that they try to arrange examinations before your consultant has even told you that you need one.

I ate my lunch while Chris got ready, helped him straighten his tie, and wished him good luck. He told me to make myself at home and pointed out all the areas of interest – the acoustic guitar in the corner of the living room, the keyboard upstairs in the library, his mountain of books. I explored all of them while he was out, feeling very much in hiding. It was a strange day, and stranger to be in his house on my own. I had a nap on the couch and woke up wondering if he had come back yet. I wandered around the house. It was big and light, with echoing floorboards and high ceilings. He wasn't home yet, so I played on the guitar some more until he returned. I hadn't played for a long time and didn't know many songs back when I did, so I was really just fooling around. I could still play The Entertainer on the keyboard, though, like I did when I was a kid. When he came back we went to the pub, where Mary would join us after work. We sat out in the pub garden and after a little while, I turned around and noticed that half of the picnic benches were unused, turned over onto their sides.

"That's weird," I said. "Why are they all on their sides like that?"

"We walked straight past those when we got here, didn't you notice them before?" Chris asked.

I had no idea why I hadn't noticed them before. I'm not the most observant person at the best of times, but maybe anxiety had turned me blind to everything else around me. Maybe I was actually going mad.

Nicola had told me to take the day off on Thursday and not worry about it, and Peter did the same at his job as an IT Technician for a group of schools. He drove me down to the hospital and we went up to the ward to tell someone we were there. A nurse told us to sit in the waiting room, and after a few nervous minutes, we were taken into a consultation room by another nurse. Then Mr Rashed appeared.

"How are you?" he asked.

"Alright. Worried about what you're going to say to me."

It wasn't good news, but we knew that. I was resigned to it at this point, and almost calm. They had found some cancerous cells in the duodenum, which is a small part of the small intestine. They were going to refer me to a hospital in Leicester, where they had specialists who dealt with the small bowel – Mr Rashed was more of an expert in the large bowel department. In the meantime, they would arrange for me to have a CT scan and the test they had called me about on Tuesday, which turned out to be something called a capsule endoscopy. Surprisingly, I left the hospital in quite good spirits. We knew what was going on, Mr Rashed had made me feel quite at ease and like whatever it was would get sorted out, and everything was going to be okay. I was very optimistic when we went to my parents' house to tell them about the appointment, and I called Nicola as well to let her know what was happening. It was as if Peter and I had had a role reversal, with me being the more laid back of the two of us for a change.

The next day was my appointment with Miss Biswas, the gynaecological consultant. These meetings took place in the maternity building at the hospital, so the waiting room was a mix of women who were pregnant and women who had something wrong with them in that department. Not a pleasant mix if you fall into the latter category. And for some reason, the clinic was always way behind schedule – at least half an hour, if you were lucky.

My dad came with me to this one. I wasn't expecting it to be anything too bad, which is why Peter wasn't there. In fact, I would have been on my own if it wasn't for my car. On Thursday evening I was about to make my way to the weekly pub quiz where I was on a team with my parents, Chris, Mary, Emma, and Zoe. But when I got outside I noticed that one of my tyres was completely flat. Not having time to do anything about it there and then, the plans for the evening, and therefore the morning, ended up changing. Peter dropped me off at the pub before going out with his friends, and I would then stay at my parents' house overnight and Dad would take me to the hospital and then to work afterwards. Then Peter would pick me up from work and we'd go home. Usually, I wouldn't have minded, but I didn't want to sleep alone in my old bed at Mum and Dad's house. I wanted to be with Peter.

I went into the consultation room the next morning by myself, not expecting to hear anything too worrying. I was there for an abscess, after all. The last thing I expected to hear was that the lining of my womb was pre-cancerous, with suspicion of early stage cancer.

That was the first time I cried in a doctor's office – I'd held it together pretty well up until then. It was all just such a shock – I mean, two cancer diagnoses in two days? How often does that happen? They asked me if I had anyone with me and I said yes, so they called my dad in and they went through everything again with him. (Had my tyre gone flat so that I wouldn't be alone at my appointment after all? I don't believe in fate or that everything happens for a reason, but it did cross my mind that the flat tyre was actually quite lucky in some ways.) Miss Biswas was going to give me another hysteroscopy, this time under general anaesthetic, and an MRI to get more information. She would also refer me and Peter to a fertility specialist in London to talk about options, but I may need to have a hysterectomy. If the cancer was early enough or if it was pre-cancer, we may be able to have a baby or freeze some eggs before any treatment or surgery happened. It was a lot to take in.

I could hardly believe it. First the news from Mr Rashed, and now this? Two diagnoses in as many days. Every time I think about it, it brings me to tears like hearing someone else's sad story. We sat in the car park and Dad asked me if I wanted to go to work or go home, and I had trouble making the decision again, but finally decided there was no point in going to work – I wasn't going to get anything done in that state. He drove me back to his house, where I cried in my mother's lap. I called Nicola to update her and let her know I wasn't coming into work, and then Peter called me to find out what was going on because I hadn't been in touch yet. He was going to finish up what he was doing at work, and then he was going to come and pick me up from Mum and Dad's and take me home. I messaged Chris and the girls, too. After I had done the digital rounds I had a phone call to arrange my capsule endoscopy for the following week. I was especially nervous about this one because I didn't know what it was going to be like. When I got off the phone, my dad made me grilled cheese on toast with chilli flakes. Real comfort food. Peter arrived to pick me up and I cried most of the way home. The memory of this day is one of the saddest and most distressing things to think about and it's something I don't like to be taken back to.

That weekend was my brother-in-law Neil's birthday party, which took place at my sister's house. Peter and I went along with my parents, and Emma and Zoe were invited, too. The whole family was there, as well as Karen and Neil's friends. Karen had arranged for a hog roast to be served, so there were staff cutting it up and serving it in the garden, and even staff serving drinks. It was very strange to come into my sister's house and be offered a drink by someone they had hired for the evening. It was a good evening though, and a chance to try to forget about things for a while. Which is of course very difficult, and it's always strange to go to scary medical appointments and try to carry on as normal when you have this massive weight in the back of your head, and everyone else knows about it too but it isn't spoken about. Walking around Aldi the day before (Peter and I wanted to try shopping somewhere new, so even this routine-but-not-routine thing felt strange), was quite similar. To have this thing happening in your body and your brain and to just be walking around like it's all fine. I felt like an alien surrounded by normal people going about their lives. I was going through the motions again, dealing with appointments and tests as best as I could with no energy left to really feel like myself. Cancer was taking over again.

On the Sunday, Peter and I continued our attempt at normality by going to see the new Han Solo movie. I think the world was really trying to distract us at this point because halfway to the cinema a thunderstorm started, accompanied by hail. It hadn't stopped raining heavily by the time we got there, and we had to park up and run into the building. After just a few seconds outside my shoes and socks were absolutely soaked. I was only wearing flimsy slip-on shoes and had opted for a hoodie rather than a coat – not that it would have made too much difference the way the rain was hammering down. I sat down in the cinema and took off my shoes and socks, hoping they would dry out a little while we watched the movie. When we got out of the cinema it had stopped raining but some of the roads were shut and parts of the town were underwater.

I decided to put my two literary magazines on hold for a while. I didn't want to give myself too much work while everything was happening (whatever "everything" turned out to be), and I didn't want to fall behind with creating the magazine or going through submissions. So I sent out emails and social media messages letting people know that I had closed to submissions until further notice.

I thought I had left the disgusting Klean-Prep drink behind now that I only had an internal pouch and not a large colon and didn't need any more colonoscopies, but apparently, I was wrong. I was sent some to take the day before my capsule endoscopy. Granted, it was only half of what a person would normally take if they had a colon because otherwise, it could make me really dehydrated, which is dangerous. I mixed it with a lot of lemon cordial and it actually turned out to not be too bad. It had a weird texture to it, but it wasn't as bad as I remembered it from the first time around. The first time, I mixed it with lime cordial, and now I would never drink that again because it would remind me of Klean-Prep. I'll probably never drink lemon juice again either, unless I have to mix it with Kean-Prep.

I worked from home on the Tuesday so that I could have my drink and go to the toilet as necessary. The other annoying part was fasting – I had lunch but then I wasn't allowed to eat anything or drink anything but water for the rest of the day. These appointments made me have to change my normal activities much more than I would have liked – I didn't want to be so rigid with my eating habits.

The following morning I went to the hospital before work. I had to swallow a tiny camera with the help of a little water, and then I could go about my day. Well, sort of. I had a big black recorder on a belt around my waist, which was pretty bulky but I sort of managed to hide it under my baggy jumper. The camera I swallowed would send data to the recorder and that's where the images would be stored. After I'd been all hooked up, I went to work. I was told I could take off the equipment once I had "passed" the camera. And no, once I had pooped out the camera, they did not want it back. It was mid-afternoon when I went to the toilet and it came out. I looked in the bowl and could see a flashing blue light where the camera was sitting. Thank goodness. Time for some food!

However, what the hospital didn't tell me was that when the recorder lost connection with the camera, it would beep several times. Loudly. I was just sitting at my desk when it started, and everyone looked around in confusion.

"Is that your phone?" my friend Jess asked.

"No," I mumbled, rushing to get up and get out of the room. "Just my... thing." It stopped beeping and I called the hospital to find out what had happened. Turns out it was all fine, and that's just what it does when the test is finished. Good to know. I went back inside as if nothing had happened, and continued to stuff my face with chocolate, relieved that now all I had to do was hand the equipment back.

Chris had been away in Wales for a week as he and Mary had been to a wedding, so I hadn't seen him since the pub quiz on the evening of my first diagnosis when I had the flat tyre. But the next Saturday night we were due some fun, in the form of a silent disco at a venue just a few minutes' walk from my flat. It was weird being the one with cancer in a group of people who had nothing of the sort, but Peter, Chris, Mary, Emma, Zoe and I had a great time that night. The silent disco involved wearing headphones which could be tuned in to your choice of three channels at any time – 80s, 90s and 00s music. It was actually the most civilised night out I'd ever been on – I could choose what I wanted to listen to, nobody could hear me singing, and there was no being knocked about or pushed against on the dancefloor. There was plenty of space for everyone. It was great to be dancing and singing and getting excited when a great song came on, but I was also glad that Chris and I found a few moments at the bar to talk about things. Though all I remember saying is that I didn't know what to say. I had no words for the awful news I had gotten and the things I had already gone through in the last couple of weeks. The silent disco was weirdly reminiscent of the night out I'd had with my friends before that first operation eight years before.

On the previous Thursday, I'd had a pre-op assessment for the hysteroscopy, which would take place the following week. The pre-op was no bother, and the hysteroscopy was relatively uneventful, too. Peter took me down and we waited in the day room on the ward for what seemed like forever. Again, it's difficult to express the anxiety and the tedium of waiting for these things. It's like waiting to go to an interview or to have your driving test, but even more scary and long. Eventually, I was seen by Miss Biswas and an anaesthetist, and I was put on a different ward where there were more beds. Peter had to leave at that point, and I spent another large chunk of time sitting around waiting to go down to theatre. It was just going to be a closer look inside the womb, so no big deal, and I wasn't too nervous about the procedure itself. I just wanted to get it over with and go home. The nurse walked me down, they got me set up in the anaesthetic room, and the last thing I remembered was the bald male anaesthetist looking down at me and saying "Now, sleep." One of the creepier ways in which someone had knocked me out, for sure.

When I came out I was put in a different ward again, and my main concern was whether the stuff I had left by my bed, including my phone, had travelled there with me. It was soon located and Peter appeared, too. The nurse gave me some toast and then I was discharged, very thankful that this time around I wasn't staying overnight in the ward. They had taken a biopsy, so it was now time for the hard part – waiting for the results.

I wasn't allowed to drive or work the next day after the anaesthetic, so as Chris was free he came to meet me at my flat and we took a little food over to the park nearby and sat under a tree in the sun. When we'd had enough of that, we walked over to the pub for a drink in the beer garden. We talked about cancer, I tried not to cry, we talked about other things – our time together was always something solid amid the madness. I was scared all the time, but there are still good times from that period that I think of fondly. Pubs, parks, silent discos, family gatherings, cinema trips, eating good food – there was often something to distract me even if I was only for a short while. There is a definite theme of needing to be distracted and appreciating all things big and small that fulfilled that duty.

There was something of a lull where nothing happened for a couple of weeks while I waited to go to my MRI and CT scan appointments. It was good to have a normal week of going to work without turning up late or having a day off due to appointments. But I was still always wary of anything coming up. I didn't want to get too comfortable in my routine because I knew that the calm wasn't going to last very long. I was still scared, and moments of positivity were just that – fleeting snatches I couldn't quite grab onto. I might have a positive thought, only for it to be replaced with something I felt was more real. Anxiety would come in waves and leave a devastation of damp in its wake like a flooded town that can never completely dry out.

It was during the lull that I received a mystery parcel. The postman tried to deliver it during the day but as Peter and I were both at work, he left a card and I had to go to the depot to collect it. I hadn't ordered anything and spent the evening musing about what it could possibly be. Had someone sent me something lovely? It turned out that yes, they had. My oldest friend Rachael, who I've known since we were four years old, sent me a BuddyBox from The Blurt Foundation. They specialise in self-care around mental health and depression, and people can either receive subscription boxes every month or order a one-off box. The one Rachael had sent to me was dinosaur themed. It contained some felt for me to sew together to make my own dinosaur, a brick dinosaur to put together, a shower bomb (like a bath bomb but it steams up your shower with lovely smells and makes it feel like a real spa), and some other lovely bits – including a very thoughtful note. I had never received a surprise package in the mail before, and it made my week. I got to work early after picking it up and I opened it at my desk, showing it with excitement to my work friend Jason.

I had my MRI scan and my CT scan, luckily both within one appointment so I didn't have to go to the hospital twice. Having the actual exams didn't make me nervous, but it was still another thing to deal with so I wasn't happy about it. And I still worried about what the outcome might be. What was the MRI going to find? What if the cancer was in more than two places? What if it was everywhere? Was I already a goner? To level out the bad with the good somehow, Peter and I would stop at Burger King on the way home from some appointments (and one time we stopped at a Chinese buffet restaurant). A little treat to make us feel a little better and take advantage of being off work for the day. It became a routine for a short while: diagnosis; burger.

While all of this was happening, the country was focusing on the World Cup, which turned out to be yet another lovely distraction for me. I don't watch much football but I do try to pay attention when the World Cup is on, so I watched most of the England games. Peter would go to the pub with his friend to watch them, and I would have them on in the background at home while I wrote. One night on the way home from work I picked up some snacks and had myself a little feast while I watched – duck spring rolls, prawn toast, chicken wontons, vegetable samosas, onion bhajis, Doritos, dip, and a bit of Easter egg to finish off with (I had some left over still as they are a particular love of mine, so I usually have lots of them that were either given to me or I bought for myself).

I did find it strange that the World Cup was happening during my diagnosis again, just as it had taken place in 2010 before my bowel surgery. Since then, I've noticed life repeating itself in other ways and worried about the cancer coming back because of a pattern I've found. Like I'll probably be worried about getting cancer again during the next World Cup. Or expect appointment letters waiting for me upon my return from holiday like when I returned from Florida. But the truth is, you can often find patterns in the things that happen if you live long enough and have any sort of structure or routine in your life. In fact, you can find patterns in everything if you look hard enough. I still need to try to stop looking.

The MRI scan came back surprisingly quickly, and soon I had an appointment to see Miss Biswas again. I was worried that it had come back so quickly – was it definitely cancer and not just pre-cancer? Was it worse than early stage? Then again, when I had to rearrange the first appointment when I came back from Florida, there were lots of slots available, so maybe they just weren't very busy and could therefore fit me in more quickly. I was trying to apply logic to the situation, but that was like trying to apply lipstick onto a swordfish.

Peter and I went to the appointment with Miss Biswas, where we found out that it was indeed cancer and not just pre-cancer – stage 1a. We were told that we could freeze some eggs for later use with a surrogate, and when that had been done I could have my womb and ovaries removed. Ovarian cancer is a risk with Lynch syndrome just like uterine cancer is, and one isn't much use without the other, so there was little point in keeping them. Having my ovaries removed would mean going into early menopause, but that sounded like something I could deal with. I had already thought about this happening. When I saw the genetic counsellor back in 2011, we talked about how I should have a hysterectomy by the age of around 35 anyway as a preventative measure because hopefully, I would have had children by then, and that's the age at which the risk of uterine cancer increases. So we already had a timer for when we

93

needed to have children by. We just didn't expect it to be cut so short. But once again, I was feeling fairly optimistic when we left. In fact, I think Miss Biswas and the key worker at the appointment were surprised at my attitude. I said it was really the best possible news I could have gotten that day, which wasn't completely true, I realised later – it being only pre-cancerous would have been better than early stage, but the outcome might have been the same either way because pre-cancerous cells couldn't just be left in there. I had been thinking about how bad it could have been and I was relieved when it was slightly better news than the worst thing that my brain could conjure up. They also said the CT scan and MRI looked okay from their point of view, so that was also good news. But what would Mr Rashed say, and how would the treatments for the two different cancers affect each other? How were the consultants going to juggle them?

Chapter Six
Can't We Just Install a Zip on Me Already?

I like to joke about cancer. My key worker in the gynaecology department had given me a form to fill in so that I could get free prescriptions, and in the summer my NHS exemption card came in the post. I showed it to Peter.

"Look at you, rinsing the system," he joked.

I told Chris about it later, and he commented: "You are deffo cheating the system, going to all this trouble for some free prescription drugs."

"I know, I think I've taken it a bit far," I agreed with a smile.

My next appointment letter came through, and it was for a gastroscopy at Leicester Royal Infirmary, which was about an hour away from where I lived in Northamptonshire. This one would be a longer, ultrasound version of the gastroscopy I'd already had, and it would take around thirty to forty minutes. Thank goodness for sedation. I panicked though, as I often did when I got an appointment letter or phone call. I didn't know if this test was standard because Mr Rashed had said he was referring me to Leicester anyway, or if it was because they had found something bad in the capsule endoscopy and needed to investigate further. By this time I was getting sick of all the tests and messing about and had sort of hoped that the next step would be some sort of operation to get rid of the polyp and have it all over and done with. But it was a complicated situation because I had two unrelated cancers in different places. The two departments had to talk to each other to decide the best way of dealing with the two problems – what surgery should be done, and which should be done first? In fact, at this point I was expecting, as I had been told in the meeting with Miss Biswas, that both surgeries would be done at the same time – slicing me open and each surgeon taking their turn before zipping me back up again. (I was also at this point joking that I should have a zip installed to make the whole thing, and any future things, a lot easier.) The morning after I received the letter, I called Mr Rashed's secretary to find out whether this test was triggered by the capsule endoscopy's findings or if it was just procedure, and to my relief, she said it was part of the procedure so that they could decide the best way to move forward. It was still rubbish to have to go through it, but I was less panicked about it in hearing it was all part of the process.

Even better was that my work friends seemed to sense that I was having a bad day and they suddenly all turned into feeders. We were having our photos taken for the website, which is quite annoying for everyone (I hate any photos of me that I didn't take myself), so to sweeten everyone up, Mary supplied Haribo and Maltesers. Extra packets of these were bestowed upon me by Mary and my "bestie", Luke. Jason also invited me to Nando's for lunch as most of the office was planning on going, but I told him that I didn't really feel like being social that day. He understood and instead he brought me a chocolate brownie back. I was so surprised and touched, and it was one of the best brownies I'd ever eaten.

The day of my gastroscopy came, and as usual, it was an afternoon of sitting around in a waiting room nervously. Luckily the sedation worked a treat, though I wished I could be sedated for the whole thing – every chat with every doctor, preferably, for however many months it was going to take. After the procedure was done, Dr Das, who was the consultant Mr Rashed had referred me to and who had carried out the gastroscopy, came to talk to me and Peter in the waiting room.

"Do you know everything?" he asked.

Well, what is everything? How the hell should we know? I thought, panicked by his serious look, the vague question and the thought of what "everything" could possibly mean.

He said that there were three cancerous polyps and that two of them could be removed but one of them was flat and therefore couldn't be removed. At the time, this made me panic because I thought he meant that surgery wasn't an option at all. What he had actually meant, I would realise later, was that he couldn't remove the flat one via the gastroscopy – so there was no point in removing two at the time if he still had to leave that one where it was. He said the polyps were very close together, and that he was going to refer me to a specialist at Leicester General Hospital. I went home with a painful stomach from the gastroscopy, too painful to finish much of my dinner so I did something unlike me and just went to bed early. I felt like I was living in a never-ending nightmare. Things were just going from bad to worse, and it was horrible updating people with what was going on. I felt like a burden on everybody, and while I wanted to keep everyone updated, it was difficult to keep going over all the little details. I kept a select few people updated, and only gave everyone else the big news. It was too much to keep repeating myself.

A couple of weeks later I had a follow-up appointment with Dr Das, in which he thankfully confirmed that he was referring me to Leicester General Hospital for a major surgery to deal with the problem. I say thankfully because during our previous encounter he had made it sound like they wouldn't be able to operate on the polyp at all. I also say thankfully because I was getting sick of people talking about things and doing tests without me feeling like we were getting any further along. As my key workers kept reminding me, it was a complicated situation and both hospitals needed to work together to decide what to do. The consultants had meetings about me in their MDTs (multi-disciplinary teams), and it sounded like I was actually becoming a little bit famous among the doctors.

The timeline for the rest of summer 2018 is a little fuzzy, but it doesn't really matter which order events happened in. To continue the theme of things going from bad to worse, Peter and I went down to London to meet the fertility specialist, Mr Farthing. I was already in London after going on a day trip with the girls and then meeting Kieran, who I hadn't seen for a few years, for drinks in the evening. Peter got the train down on his own and we met up later to go to the hotel we had booked. The next day we would get the tube to the hospital, where we would arrive early (I arrive early for pretty much everything) and proceed to sit in the absolutely packed waiting room for an hour and a half, waiting for our delayed appointment. I've never seen a waiting room so busy – people were standing around because there weren't enough chairs for everyone who was waiting. Goodness knows what the delay was that made the clinic run so far behind. Add to that, it was late July and there was no air conditioning. We were packed in and roasting, and I was getting quite cranky about the whole thing.

When we finally got in, Mr Farthing proved to be very friendly and knowledgeable. He was pretty much up to speed with my situation, though as always I had to clarify a few things about my medical history. Always fun to recount those details. But what Mr Farthing told us came as a bit of a surprise. We thought we were there to discuss fertility options – mainly, freezing my eggs for future use with a surrogate. To get this procedure underway I would first need to take medication to make me fertile, which would happen a couple of weeks before egg collection. But Mr Farthing explained that stimulating the eggs also results in stimulation of the lining of the womb. In other words, it would cause the lining of the womb to grow, and this might also make the cancer grow faster. We could still do it, but it was up to me to decide if I wanted to take the risk. I didn't. Which was good in a way because as he said, when a patient doesn't want to take any risks it makes the whole decision process easier for everyone, and they can just do whatever is best for the patient. Mr Farthing did also present us with another option – an alternative to surgery. This would be in the form of medication that changes the hormones in the body, and it can work when the cancer has been caused by a hormonal imbalance. But as mine was caused by Lynch syndrome, there wasn't any evidence as to whether or not it would work for me. And this treatment would take a year, so at the end of it we'd be a year on and if it hadn't worked, the cancer might have spread. So that was a risk, too. And leaving the ovaries would put me at risk of ovarian cancer from Lynch syndrome, so we discussed removing them at the same time as removing the womb. Peter and I agreed we didn't want to take any unnecessary risks. So no risks for us. And no biological children for us. Even if we did opt for IVF, the chances of it working would have been extremely low.

I figured that the concept of not having my own children was something I would deal with later. I felt guilty that I couldn't give Peter children because I knew he wanted them – probably more than I did. I had never been one of those women who were desperate to be a mother. I always thought that if it happened, then that would be great and I was sure I'd be very excited. But if it didn't happen, it wouldn't be the end of the world for me. I wasn't ready to process it all, anyway, and after already experiencing bowel surgery and the emotional trauma that came long after, I knew that I probably wouldn't feel the true upset of the situation until much later.

We now knew that we were opting for surgery, but surgery still comes with risks. More so with me because of my previous surgery. The womb and the bowel are quite close to each other and there was a chance that various organs in that crowded area of the body might be stuck together. It would therefore be a good idea to have a bowel surgeon present just in case things went wonky during surgery – we didn't want anything to happen to my internal pouch, which had been working brilliantly so far. So even though we had chosen a course of action, it was all still quite worrying.

I was sent for a PET scan after this, which is a bit like a CT scan except the dye they inject you with in this case contains radioactive tracers. The aim was to see my insides in more detail so they could better plan my surgery and make sure they were doing the right thing. Peter took me to the hospital in our town (the fourth hospital we'd be referred to in our grand tour of nearby medical institutes). I was put in a small room and given the injection. I then had to stay in there by myself for an hour while the injection got to work. There were no reading materials (so that germs and infections aren't transmitted between patients who read them, apparently) and the only thing of interest in the room was a CD player and a copy of the Bridget Jones' Diary soundtrack someone had picked up at a charity shop. I didn't put it on, so had to be content with my own thoughts for a while. After the hour was up I went in for the scan, which was quite peaceful and I even drifted off to sleep a bit at one point. I woke up when my leg jerked slightly in my sleep, then tried to stay awake for the rest of the time because the scan wouldn't be much good if I was moving about. The scan was done and I was free to go — though advised not to hang around with small children or pregnant women for eight hours while I was still radioactive. I wondered if I might gain a superpower.

The next appointment was with my new consultant, Mr Bhardwaj at Leicester General. The waiting room was huge and full of people waiting to go into different clinics. We were directed into a small room that had just one trolley in it and no chairs. The nurse told me to lie down.

"Lie down?" I asked in confusion. I wasn't expecting to be examined. "What for?"

"He said to get you to lie down," she said. So I did, reluctantly.

A man came into the room and introduced himself. He wasn't Mr Bhardwaj, but he was on the surgical team.

"Shall we get this moved so you can sit up a bit?" he said, looking at the trolley. I swung my legs off and sat on the edge of it, and the man went off to get Mr Bhardwaj.

"Why did she tell me to lie down?" I said to Peter, then immediately clammed back up when he gestured that she was in the adjoining room, the door to which was wide open. I was annoyed and embarrassed and we hadn't even started yet.

We had taken an hour-long drive to the hospital for an appointment which felt sort of like something of a meet-and-greet, and a general debunking of some of the assumptions we had in our heads based on what we had been told by other consultants so far. No, they probably wouldn't do both procedures at the same time because the operation for my duodenal cancer would be too big, and putting them together would be too much of a strain for me. So we were now looking at two separate operations – probably the hysterectomy first as it was smaller, and then this second operation once I had recovered from that. The second operation was called a Whipple procedure. I had never heard of it.

"Is it a bigger or smaller operation than having your bowel removed?" I asked.

"Definitely bigger," the key worker and Mr Bhardwaj both said. I was taken aback. I couldn't imagine having an operation that was even bigger than the one I'd had eight years ago.

Even though I would now be having two separate operations, they still wanted me to have both of them at Leicester, rather than having the Whipple there and the hysterectomy closer to home in Kettering. They said it was easier for everything to be under one roof so that the consultants could easily communicate with each other about my case. The next thing for me to do was to go and see Mr Davies, who would be doing my hysterectomy. The date was set for 12th September, with a pre-op appointment a week or so before. Things were finally happening, and although I was scared that something might go wrong with either operation, I was just relieved that we had a plan and the sooner we got on with it, the sooner it would all be over.

One of the things that annoyed me about surgery was the preparation. You couldn't just not think about it until the day and then go. At the pre-op appointment, I was given odourless shower gel (that annoyingly didn't lather up) to use for the three days before my surgery, including that morning. This was to ward off MRSA. I also had some anti-septic cream to put in my nostrils three times a day for those three days. And I was given four small pre-op drinks. I had to drink two before bed the night before, and two in the morning. They were fine – around 200ml each and they tasted of lemon. So on the morning of the surgery, I had to get up early to shower with this non-lathering substance and drink two of those drinks, then ride in the car for an hour to get to the hospital at around seven-thirty. Obviously, I needed to go to the toilet halfway there because of the drinks, so we were cutting it fine time-wise by the time we had located a McDonald's and made a stop.

At the hospital, we sat in yet another crowded room and waited for my name to be called, then we went into a room where a nurse asked me the usual pre-op questions and got a bit of background from me. She was surprised to hear about my diagnoses.

"Have you ever had breast cancer?" she asked.

"Not yet," I said.

"Oh don't say that, you're so young."

Unfortunately, youth hadn't done me many favours so far.

At this point, Peter had to leave, so I gave him a worried goodbye and went into a long ward where I would get into my hospital gown and pyjamas, give a urine sample, and then sit and wait some more. I was seen by an anaesthetist and by Mr Davies, but apart from that I just had to wait for a nurse to come and get me. I had brought a book with me but I couldn't concentrate on reading – I kept hoping I would be the next person to be taken away. The radio was playing old pop songs that I didn't really like, and I longed for Radio 1.

Finally, my turn came and a nurse walked me down to the theatre. It was a big hospital, and I followed her downstairs and through several corridors. We got to the theatre area and sat down together to wait some more, for someone in the surgical team to come out and say they were ready for me. I was so nervous I was shaking, and the woman who came out to get me kindly took me by the arm as she led me to the anaesthetic room, and said they would look after me. The kindness of the people working for the NHS was always invaluable to me.

It was almost time to go under, but first, they had to put a cannula in my hand and draw some blood from me. One of the men in there asked me to drop my hand and then squeezed my arm in an attempt to wake up the vein.

"I feel like a tube of toothpaste," I said. They laughed. I was the patient making the anaesthetists laugh right before they put me under. Where would we be without humour in those darkest moments?

Compared to my bowel operation, this one wasn't too bad. I woke up in pain and drowsy but relieved to have woken up at all. My parents, my sister, Peter and Chris all came to visit me, with my parents and Peter coming every day – though I felt bad that they had travelled so far to see me and I could barely stay awake to talk to them, especially later in the evening. My catheter was taken out on the second day of my stay, which surprised and worried me. It meant I had to get up and go to the toilet now, and that I had to make an effort to walk around and get better. Plus, once we were up and about we were expected to go to the kitchen and sort out our own breakfast. We had toast, cereal, fruit and yoghurt to choose from. I would have much rather had breakfast brought to me at my bed. It was a good thing really, though, because walking around helps to get your bowels working again, and going to the toilet was something of a pre-requisite to leaving the hospital. I had to leave a urine sample in the bathroom to show that I was peeing enough and that I didn't have a water infection, and I had to have a bowel movement before they let me go. In the small four-bed ward I was in, each of us celebrated when we managed to do each of these things – ticking off requirements that took us closer to going home. And I was certainly keen to get home. Once again I had the problem of finding it difficult to lie on my side, but I found that I could sort of prop myself up with the help of a pillow placed behind my back. I was looking forward to the comfort of my own bed.

I was in the hospital for just three days this time around, but I nearly didn't get out on the day that I wanted to. Discharges happened in the afternoons or early evenings, so when Mr Davies came on his rounds and we talked about going home, he said to see how I got on that day. But when a nurse came around to do my observations in the afternoon, my temperature was slightly high. That could be a sign of infection. I had to do another urine sample and wait nervously for my observations to be done again an hour later. I willed my temperature to go down, and when the nurse came back to check it, it was back to normal. I could go home. I was given some syringes so that I could inject myself with something called Fragmin, which is used to prevent DVT when people aren't moving around much. The nurses did it for me every day in hospital, but when I got home I had to get used to stabbing myself in the leg for the next month or so.

Peter picked me up from the hospital. The journey back home was bumpy and painful, as all car journeys would be for the next few weeks. Before we went home, we stopped at Peter's mum's house and I waited in the car while he went inside. He emerged a few minutes later with two colourful wicker baskets with long handles, adorned with pink plastic flowers. They were full of treats like fudge, mints, little cups of jelly, chocolate wafer bars, and more. And there was an additional shopping bag filled with more things Peter's mum, Denise, had picked up at the shops for us. It was very thoughtful – the last thing either of us wanted to do when we got home was think about food shopping. In fact, during the time while I was recovering, we began getting our supermarket food delivered instead and it made life so much easier.

It was a tough recovery at home. I had been throwing up in the hospital and my pouch was trying to get over the shock of being moved around. For the first couple of days, it was like I'd had my colostomy reversal all over again. I had bad wind pain and acid reflux, and couldn't face eating very much. My belly hurt and I was too tired to do anything but sit and watch TV. Even picking up my phone to reply to my friends' messages felt like too much effort. I felt awful, and couldn't see an end to my misery. I felt like I was going to die, and that maybe it would be a relief if I did.

Food wasn't the only thing I had given to me. My friends sent get well cards and flowers – we had three big bunches in the house at one point, one of them being sent by my work colleagues. Peter's friend (another Chris) and his wife sent me a big Cadbury's chocolate hamper – my favourite. Now, that was an exciting thing to get in the mail! Emma, Rachael and Zoe clubbed together to send me another package. This one contained some chocolate, some bath bombs which smelled fruity enough to eat, and a little beanbag designed to sit on my lap so that I could rest my tablet on my belly without hurting myself.

It was a few weeks after that when I found the website they had probably got the idea from for that last gift – and it turned out Peter had been on that website, too. One evening after another day of pain and wind and acid reflux, I had what I think was my first migraine. My head didn't hurt but my vision went really strange. We were watching television and suddenly everything was a bit blurry as if my eyes had a wavy line in front of them. It was quite startling as I'd never experienced anything like it before. Peter reassured me that it would probably go away soon, but in the meantime, I needed to do something that didn't involve using my eyes. I put my headphones on, leaned back in my armchair, and listened to some music from a past life. Suddenly, when I put The Killers' first album on, it wasn't 2018 anymore. It was 2005 and I was at a friend's house party. I was sitting in the dining room surrounded by people I liked and who seemed to like me too, and we were singing along to Mr Brightside at the tops of our voices. I let myself well up a bit at the memory of such an easier time – almost eighteen years old and still in sixth form, with no idea of what was to come. To my mind and with the benefit of hindsight, there was just happiness and very little pain there (except when boys were involved).

Returning to 2018, I opened my eyes because I could suddenly smell lemons very strongly. Was Peter cleaning the kitchen? He wasn't. He had bought an essential oils diffuser – a little wooden thing with a spout at the top, which was now sitting on the coffee table and emitting steam, along with the refreshing smell of lemongrass. He had bought it to cheer me up – and, as the website I later found said, to help me to de-stress. I knew that he did a lot of research around my condition, surgery, various symptoms and the things the consultants said, but I hadn't expected this. I explored the website (livebetterwithmenopause.com) myself and found lots of great tips and ideas for products that can help with symptoms during the menopause. The smells from the diffuser were a little waft of joy.

Slowly we started going for little walks. I went from wandering around our tiny flat in circles, to going around the block, to walking the few minutes to our local pub. A week or two after I was discharged, we went to see Mr Davies. He was happy with my progress and said he was going to hand me over to Mr Bhardwaj, letting him know that I was ready for my second operation. I was worried about the effect that a second operation might have on my body, but I was once again keen to get it over with. The other takeaway from our meeting was that I didn't need any further treatment – the cancer hadn't spread anywhere else, and I was being referred back to Miss Biswas at Kettering hospital to talk at a later date about whether I should go on HRT for the effects of the menopause. It was a couple of weeks before I started feeling the effects of the menopause, and this only really came in the form of the odd hot flush. I wasn't too worried about it.

The strange thing was, I hadn't had any abscesses since I was referred to Mr Doshi at the beginning of the year. This thing that had plagued me for months suddenly went away once I went for the MRI. It was as if it had existed only to prompt me to seek medical help, and once I was on my way to having my cancer diagnosed, its job was done. Like my body was trying to tell me something. I don't really believe in that kind of thing, and I certainly don't believe in fate or that everything happens for a reason. My general philosophy is that things just happen, and sometimes they are good and sometimes they're terrible. There's no reason or rhyme for it. But in this case, it was certainly strange that the initial problem disappeared as soon as I found out what the larger problem was.

I was also very lucky that Mr Doshi had changed his mind about sending me for a hysteroscopy. I should have said yes to it myself because I knew what the risks were with Lynch syndrome, but I was so scared of what they might find. If I hadn't had the abscess, the consultant wouldn't have sent me for an MRI, and I wouldn't have been referred to Mr Doshi because of what the MRI picked up. And if Mr Doshi hadn't then sent me for a hysteroscopy, I wouldn't have had my cancer diagnosis and you'd be sat here reading a memoir written by a ghost from beyond the grave. (Because of course, I'll still be writing when I'm a ghost.) It's just amazing how everything lined up to get me on the right track – even if at the time it felt like a terrible track to be on.

Peter took a week off work to be with me for the first few days I was home. Then when he had to go back to work, I spent my days at my parents' house until I was happy to be left on my own. When I was able to drive again I took myself to my parents' house a couple of days a week so that I didn't go completely stir crazy being in the flat by myself all day.   There was no point going back to work and taking all of my clients back from the people who I'd handed them over to because I'd only need to give them back again a couple of weeks later. We went back to Leicester to see Mr Bhardwaj again and had a long meeting with him and my extremely helpful key worker. The date for the next operation was set for 7th November.

I was even more scared this time around than I was for the hysterectomy. It was a much bigger operation and involved re-routing my digestive system. They would be removing my duodenum, the head of the pancreas, the gallbladder and the bile duct, and then sewing together what was left. This meant that my parts of my digestive system would be in a different order once they were done. I was warned how tough it was going to be to recover from this one. My key worker said it can take six months or even a year for people to feel like their normal selves again. I would have another scar, this time going across my abdomen, just below the ribs. The other two operations both left vertical scars (luckily it only really looks like one scar as the incisions were made so close together), so I was going to be left with something of a T-shape on my belly, with a little dash to the left of it, which was the two-inches or so scar from where my stoma used to be. I quite liked that one as it was really just like a big dimple. I hated my belly though as it was already misshapen, with one side of it sticking out slightly more than the other. Plus, the removal of my bowel meant that the bottom part of my belly was completely flat, which made the upper half stick out even more. These were all cosmetic concerns though, of course. The main thing I was worried about was being killed during the operation (there was a 5% chance of this happening, I was told), or if I did survive it, recovery being absolutely horrendous. The latter was the lesser of two evils I supposed, but either way you looked at it, things were pretty terrible. I'd already had one recent operation and didn't know how I was going to cope mentally, or how I'd cope physically, with having another one. However, the key worker told me that it wasn't unusual for people to have multiple operations on close-by areas of the body within this kind of time frame. And if elderly people could withstand having a Whipple procedure, I figured surely I could, too. The surgery would require me to spend between one to three days in the high-dependency unit (HDU), and then around a week or so in a regular ward. We were allowed to go and have a quick look at the unit so that we knew what to expect before my operation. A bit like viewing a house you are thinking of buying, I suppose. HDU is similar to intensive care and it was on the same ward – the difference is that in the ICU there is one nurse to every patient, and in the HDU there is one nurse for every two patients. Those in the ICU need a little more attention.

I had a couple of weeks until the operation, so I went on a couple of trips in between. The first was a trip to Canterbury with Chris. We went to some great restaurants (one Asian restaurant and one steak house), took a trip to Herne Bay (including a very cold walk in the wind three miles up the coast to Reculver), and walked around Canterbury Cathedral. The following weekend, Peter and I spent two nights in Great Yarmouth. It was almost as cold as Canterbury, and to reflect that, many places were shut – to our disappointment, the restaurant we usually went to was closed, and to my discomfort, the toilets on the beach were shut, too. Luckily most of the arcades were still open, but we made a mental note to not go quite so out of season next time. I was just happy that I was capable of standing around in an arcade for a couple of hours, and that I had managed a total of six miles walking at

Herne Bay with no problems. The only black cloud was the knowledge that soon I would once again be unable to sit upright in a chair for very long, let alone go on nice trips.

It was time for my pre-op assessment, which was fairly straight forward but this time involved having an ECG to make sure my heart was ready for the challenge of big surgery, too. I was given the same things again – the anti-MRSA shower gel, the nose cream, the lemon drinks. Luckily this time I was asked to drink all four drinks the day before, so there would be no toilet stops on the way this time.

As if to prove that things weren't quite over on the gynaecological side of things, I had an appointment with Miss Biswas two days before my Whipple procedure. However, this follow-up appointment turned out to be with someone else from the team, who I hadn't met before. She didn't even seem to know that I'd had a hysterectomy. We talked about whether I should go on HRT, and she said this would be discussed by the MDT because it comes with a small cancer risk. The consultant also told me how brave and strong and amazing I was, to be going through all of this without complaining, and still smiling. I wondered how she could know that when she had only known me for five minutes, but she said many other patients would complain about much smaller problems. I still disagreed with the "strong and brave" appraisal because I didn't see that there was any other option. But it was sort of nice to hear that I was somehow a better breed of patient, or that perhaps my general optimism was still apparent, even if I didn't feel particularly optimistic at the time.

When we got to the hospital on the day of my surgery, we discovered that all the other people being admitted for surgery in my particular batch were men, so I was given a side room all to myself – including my own toilet. Later I would wish that I could have a side room for my entire stay, but I was only in there for a couple of hours while I waited to be taken down to surgery. Luckily, this time Peter could stay with me right up until it was time to go.

Chapter Seven
The Too-Long Hospital Stay

Of all the fuzzy parts of my story, the first few days after my Whipple procedure are certainly some of the fuzziest. I remember the anaesthetic room being full (very full, this time) of lovely, friendly and professional people again. I don't remember drifting off and I don't remember waking up. I do sort of remember someone saying something about a chest x-ray and helping me to sit up, which hurt a lot. I remember lying in bed in the HDU, where the nurse stood at the end of my bed making notes. Peter tried to look at the notes and got told off by one member of staff. ("Those notes are for doctors only.") Peter and my parents came to see me every day. Chris came to see me in the HDU but had a holiday booked for that week. He continued to voice his concern for me from the beach at Gran Canaria. My friend Jess, who had been a work colleague until fairly recently, had apparently sent me a message asking if she could come and see me on the Sunday, and I had replied saying yes. She had then replied asking where I was and when she could come, but I must have forgotten completely about her correspondence because I didn't reply. It wasn't until I had been home for a week or two that I looked on Facebook Messenger and saw her messages, and I realised I had accidentally ignored her. I could barely remember being in the HDU at all, let alone using my phone while I was in there, and must have spent most of it in a drugged-up haze. It was probably best left that way. I had read that some people who were in the ICU or HDU for long periods found it very upsetting, and even had PTSD from being in there. I remember crying because a man (I can't remember who he was) told me that I needed to breathe more deeply and use my lungs properly otherwise I was going to get a chest infection. I burst into tears and he apologised a lot, but I wasn't crying just because of what he said. I was a bit, because as far as I knew I was breathing and I couldn't breathe very deeply anyway – it *hurt*. If I was going to get a chest infection, it was clearly going to be my fault but there also wasn't much I felt I could do about it. I couldn't deal with other people having such high expectations as to expect me to breathe properly. I was probably also crying because of the whole situation. And once I started, I was embarrassed to be crying in front of strangers, though they probably saw it all the time, and it was perfectly reasonable for me to be upset. I was in for three days, and then on Friday night, I was moved to a regular ward.

The ward I was put on was huge. I'd never been in any ward like it – they pushed my bed down the ward and I watched as we went past bed after bed after bed. I was used to staying in small rooms with four or six beds altogether. We finally got to my slot at the other end of the ward, but as I found out later, some of my things got left behind at the HDU – my toothbrush and my deodorant. Nothing that couldn't easily be replaced, but it was rather annoying when I couldn't have a proper shower and needed any way to feel slightly more human. Those first few days on the ward were also a little fuzzy, and just like after my hysterectomy, I was falling asleep all the time, even with visitors. This time around, my visitors included my sister and my niece and nephew, as well as my Aunty Stella (Mick's wife and my dad's sister) and my cousin Michelle, who drove down together all the way from Manchester to come and see me. The ward wasn't too loud, except for one elderly woman who would shout out, day or night, worried about not being looked after or the nurses hurting her, or talking to members of her family who weren't there. She reminded me of a woman who I had shared a ward with when I had my bowel removed – she would shout out for help, shout that she was dying, that they were trying to hurt her. It was very distressing to hear, and then one morning she was gone. I didn't know where she went.

The morning after I got moved to the big ward, I was taken for a CT scan. I think this was to check for the previously mentioned chest infection, and it was a bit of an ordeal. I mean, just having to get out of bed was an ordeal in itself. I was wheeled down in a chair, which was something quite new to me, having only been in a wheelchair that first time in A&E. Then of course once we were down there I had to get out of the chair and lie down to go through the scanner, and then get up and back on the chair, be wheeled back up, and get back into bed. As anyone who has had abdominal surgery will probably understand, all of this is very difficult when you feel like you've been sawn in half and stitched back together. I got back to find that lunch had arrived – soft food only for me, so just yoghurt – but there was no spoon. I wanted to be as little of a nuisance as possible, so I hated it when I had to ask a nurse for something so basic when they were so busy. I was not having a good day. The next day the doctors on their rounds told me there were signs of a chest infection on the CT scan results, so I was put on antibiotics. (Mr Bhardwaj told me a couple of days later that CT scans do sometimes seem to show that a patient has signs of a chest infection but it may in fact not really be the case, so I was never sure if I actually did have a chest infection.)

I had all sorts of tubes and things coming out of me in the HDU. One of them was a tube that went up my nose, down my throat and into my stomach. It was quite uncomfortable and because it was taped to my nose, it felt ridiculous – like a very thin elephant trunk. I was very glad to be rid of it when they eventually took it out. I was allowed to sip water, and then the next day move onto liquid food, and then solid. But as my throwing up continued, it was decided that I should go back to liquids for a while because perhaps my stomach couldn't handle solid food yet. I wanted to argue it – I certainly didn't want to take what felt like a step backwards. I wanted to get better and go home. But it was of course for the best, and I was back on solid food just a day or two later.

When you're in hospital the day is so very structured, and I started to try to plan my movements based on what was due to happen. For example, I didn't want to be in the toilet when my doctors were doing the rounds, so I waited until they had been and gone. I didn't want to miss the woman coming around taking lunch and dinner orders either, so I tried to be around for that. Not that there were many other places I could be – there was the bathroom, the day room, and that was about it. One morning, a volunteer came around offering hand massages, which I accepted mainly for the novelty of it. Another day, a volunteer came around just to talk to some of us, so we had someone to chat to for a few minutes. I hadn't had any of this during my previous hospital stays, and it was appreciated. Not least because the mornings felt like the longest part of the day. That time between breakfast and lunch, very little happened, and visiting time didn't start until 2pm. I often had a nap in the morning, but I didn't like waking up just before lunch, because then I would feel too groggy to eat.

My belly was quite painful, despite trying to manage it with morphine. For all three of my major operations, I had a morphine pump which I could use myself – I just had to press the button and it worked, and there was no way for me to give myself too much. I didn't have an epidural this time, but I had a wound infusion instead. According to the anaesthetist who saw me, this was an "old school" method of pain relief, which didn't fill me with optimism, but he said it would work so I trusted him. Unfortunately, sometimes these things leak and need to be removed, and after a few days, that's what happened with mine.

I also had some problems with my cannula. It had to be taken out because there was something wrong with it, and I was then on oral pain medication only. I didn't know how I would make it through the night without my morphine. My cannula was taken out and put back in several times, and the more times it happened and the more blood tests I had, the fewer places there were to try putting it in. Several people tried to put it in, and of course, it hurt every time. One doctor came to see me in the middle of the night and tried to fit the cannula in. He asked what I did for fun and I said I was a writer. He said maybe he would end up in one of my stories as the nasty doctor who woke me up and hurt me, but he couldn't have been more lovely. Shame I can't remember his name, or anyone's for that matter.

At one point, the cannula was put in my foot because my hands and arms were simply no good for it – it was making my hands swell up, and I usually loved my hands. My legs, ankles and feet were swollen, too – my body was almost unrecognisable to me. Having the cannula in my foot felt very odd, but apparently, I wasn't the first person to have one placed there. It didn't stay there for very long. Eventually, someone else came along and managed to put the needle in my hand, no problem, and there it stayed until I went home.

Another strange thing I discovered after surgery was that I had some numbness in my hands – mainly my fingers. Mr Bhardwaj told me this can happen after surgery sometimes and was something to do with if they had hit a nerve. Slowly the pins and needles went away, starting with my pinky fingers and eventually going away in my forefingers and thumbs, but it didn't fully go away until a couple of months after surgery.

After a few days on the big ward, I was moved to a smaller side room with four beds, which is where I was for the remainder of my stay. Someone was coming up from ICU who needed more attention than I did, so they were being put on the larger ward where they could be kept an eye on. The other patients in this smaller room included one I had seen around before, and who seemed to be quite well known with patients and staff. My bed on the large ward was next to a side room where one girl around my age was staying. She was in a wheelchair and seemed to be friends with the girl on my new ward, who was also my age. I'd see them going past my bed together quite often. The girl on my new ward was called Katie and she was lovely. She wore a leopard print dressing gown which gaped to reveal a large chest tattoo –

something with wings, I think. She walked with a cane and had long, curly blonde hair. She was always either going back and forth with her friend to sit at each other's beds or going downstairs for a smoke or to sit in the café. Or she was sleeping. Some days she would sleep until mid-afternoon, only waking up when she was brought food. Nurses were always looking for her and asking where she was so that they could do her observations. I couldn't blame her for wandering about, though – she had been in hospital for five weeks by the time I left. If I was there for that long, I would be going crazy.

In fact, after a week, I was more than ready to go, so I started having a little wander around myself. When my parents came to visit me, we walked down to the café for a snack. It turned out it was actually quite a long walk for me (about five minutes) and as it was painful for me to just sit upright at the table, it was a very tiring expedition. But it was a little exciting, too. The café was actually really nice – big and modern looking with lots of food options. Of course, I couldn't take advantage of most of the food as my appetite was so small, but I did have a very good flapjack – half then and half later. It was just nice to be in a room that wasn't full of beds and other sick people and people who wanted to check my blood pressure. This was where my parents and Peter spent so much time waiting for me to have had my operations. Months later in the flat, I would stumble across one of those loyalty cards you get stamped every time you buy something from the café. Peter had three stamps and was just another three away from getting a free coffee.

One day when I was in the smaller room, I decided I was going to have a proper shower, instead of just a wash down at the sink. It seemed like it would be easier, that I should probably do it, and that it might make me feel better, especially to wash my hair. But quite quickly, I wished I hadn't bothered. The shower cubicle didn't have a proper handle – it had a sort of lip on the outside, which I used to pull the door open. I got inside, and found washing and shampooing a little difficult because there wasn't anywhere to put my shampoo and shower gel while I washed. After an awkward attempt, I decided I was done and tried to open the door. It wouldn't budge. The shower was obviously wet and slippery, and I was feeling very delicate and didn't want to use too much force in case I hurt myself. I used as much force as I could – both ways, because I couldn't remember if I needed to push or pull – but I couldn't get it open. I was stuck in the shower. There was an emergency cord dangling from the ceiling, so I pulled on it and waited. Nobody came. I pushed down the panic rising in my stomach and began shouting and banging on the shower door. It was just a couple of minutes before a nurse came, but it felt like too long. I was so scared nobody would hear me. I was worried about getting cold, and not being able to stand up for very long, and being stuck in there all day – or even, as my mind began to race, dying in there, trapped with no-one knowing where I was.

"I'm stuck in the shower, the door won't open," I called. The nurse tried the door but I had locked it (which she complained about later – but of course I had locked it. I didn't want anyone to come in while I was naked, did I?) She came in and pulled the shower door open.

"Are you okay?"

"Yeah, I'm fine," I said, grabbing my towel to protect my modesty. She left me to get dressed and I tried not to feel too embarrassed, though I wondered how many other people had heard me shouting. I was amazed that nobody had had a problem with the door before – what good was a door with no handle, which seemed to have some sort of suction on it, for infirm people like me and the others on the ward? I was more annoyed than embarrassed, though for a moment there I had been a little scared.

I was having trouble sleeping because once again it was difficult to find a good position. In fact, it was pretty much impossible. Not only could I not lie on my side very well, even with a pillow propping up my back, but lying on my back wasn't comfortable either. I would be constantly up and down in the night – adjusting the bed, moving the pillows, changing positions. At one point I even fell asleep in the chair next to my bed, which I was often in and out of. I should have been resting but I just couldn't get comfortable enough to keep still. The nights were so long. By the time Friday came, I was desperate to go home just to get some sleep.

One night during the time I was writing this book, I had a dream that I was in hospital. A woman who was on the consultant's team came around to see me, but I couldn't hear what she was saying very well because it was so loud all around us, I think with people talking. She told me that I was doing really well and that I could go home soon. At first, I thought (hoped) she meant that day, but she said Friday. I asked what day it was today and she said Wednesday. (There was also a man hiding in the bathroom next to my bed. I'm not sure what he was doing in there but I was worried that he would tell people something he knew about me – something I had done that I shouldn't have, perhaps. That bit isn't really important, but is a good example of the kind of strange dreams I have, with elderly, bearded and possibly homeless men hiding in strange places.) Whatever it meant, that dream stuck with me as I woke up and went about my morning. It might have been because I was writing about my experiences and spending so much time thinking about cancer, or it might have been because I had two follow-up appointments that week. It wasn't the first of these dreams and it certainly wouldn't be the last. It's just another example of how cancer stays with you even when you don't have it anymore.

It's also an example of how I remember things without realising. Because after I had the dream, I was looking through some messages to my friends and I found a message I'd sent on the Wednesday where I had said: "Just keen to get home, hopefully Friday apparently". I thought that my brain had conjured up Wednesday and Friday by itself. I had no idea that I had actually been told on the Wednesday that I would probably be going home on the Friday. I didn't remember that at all, but my subconscious must have.

Unfortunately, Friday came around and my departure wasn't as certain as I hoped it would be. In the morning the doctors did the rounds and I was told that I would be able to go home that evening as long as my blood test came back okay. After a lot of anxious waiting around on my part, the phlebotomist came to do my blood test late morning. So when my parents came to visit me that afternoon, we envisioned them taking me back home in time for dinner. To kill some time, I asked if we could go for a look around the hospital just to get out of the ward, but if this time I could go in a wheelchair. So my parents took me for a tour around the rather large hospital. I had been hoping that there was some sort of garden we could sit in because I remembered visiting my grandad once in hospital, somewhere in Manchester, and we sat with him on a bench in a nice little garden. I imagined that must have been a nice change for him after being stuck in bed. But there was no such thing here. We had a little look around the gift shop, where I bought a thank you card for the nurses on the ward. Dad pushed me around in the chair – I was a little afraid at times that we were going to crash into someone with a bed or trolley coming the other way. It was strange to worry about bumping into someone or something and not be in a position to stop it.

I had been having some trouble with acid reflux, but I could usually figure out when I was going to just burp and when I was going to burp up sick. Unfortunately, a high-speed tour of the hospital is perhaps not the best idea when you're not feeling great. We went outside for a couple of minutes so I could see some actual daylight and get some fresh air for the first time in a week and a half. And that's when I threw up – some of it into a tissue I was holding, but some on my brand new, clean grey jumper I had put on to go home. And a bit on the ground, when I finally managed to direct it elsewhere. We tried to clean it up but it looked like I'd spilt soup down myself. I hoped nobody would notice and think I wasn't fit to go home because I had been sick.

We had packed up all of my stuff into my two bags except for the puzzle book I was still using and the box of chocolates I was working my way through. My cannula had been taken out and I was free of everything sticky or with wires. The pharmacist had been around to check what medication I needed. The only thing we could do now was wait for my blood test to come back and for my discharge paperwork to be put together.

Time edged on and it got to early evening. We asked the nurses what was happening. My parents were going to hang around until we found out whether the blood test was okay and I could go home, but the nurses were still waiting around to hear from the consultants and they couldn't tell us anything more. Visiting time ended at 8pm and my parents were still there, with no idea of whether or not they were taking me home. My mum and I went into the day room for a little while to get a change of scenery, and to test if the chairs in there were any more comfortable for me. They were, a little, but the room was very warm and painted a shocking bright yellow that almost made me feel a bit sick to look at. We talked and I had a little cry out of frustration. I had already been through so much, and it looked like it still wasn't over. I just wanted to go home, and I had been feeling anxious all day about whether it was actually going to happen. I had half a mind to discharge myself if they wouldn't let me go. It wasn't prison, after all. But I knew it wasn't a good idea, really.

My dad and I went to the nurse's station to ask again if they knew anything. I had been cold so I was wandering around in my dad's dark red V-neck jumper. As we were about to approach, the phone rang and we listened to the half of the conversation we could hear. It didn't sound good.

"So can she go home? No?" The nurse looked at my desperate, pleading face. "Are you going to come down here and tell her that, then?" she asked, as if the person on the other end of the phone was too chicken to give me the news himself. "We've already told ICU they could have the bed." She hung up and looked over at us.

"No, I can't, I can't stay here another night," I had been mumbling while she was on the phone.

"The doctor is saying that your white blood cell count is a little low and because that can be a sign of infection, he isn't happy to send you home. He is going to get a second opinion from someone more senior."

We waited to hear back from the doctors again, but there were no more phone calls. After 9pm we decided that mum and dad should go home and leave me there, as much as I didn't want them to. I didn't want to be on my own and I didn't want to stay there. I kept my dad's jumper on over my nightie and it made me feel a tiny bit better. If I had my knee-high boots on I thought I might look a bit like Ariana Grande (pfft, in my dreams). I went to bed and to my amazement, managed to get a couple hours' sleep in a semi-comfortable position.

The next day brought even more anxiety. It was a Saturday, which meant that everything was slightly quieter and a little off-kilter. Doctors didn't go on their rounds until much later than they did on weekdays. It was the second day in a row that I didn't want to go to the toilet for fear of missing someone coming around to talk to me. Eventually, the doctors came around, led by one of my favourite young consultants whose name I didn't know.

"You're doing really well," he said.

"I shouldn't still be here."

"Yeah, I heard that."

He asked the nurse how much fluid had been coming out of my surgical drain – I had one left but the other two had already been removed. The drains were tubes that had been inserted into my stomach and had bags attached to them to catch excess fluid coming out of where I'd had my surgery. A trainee nurse had taken them out. I was a little alarmed when I heard she had never done it before, but of course, all the staff have to start somewhere, so I agreed to be a test dummy for her. She seemed to do it perfectly.

"We'll send you home with that drain still in, and you can come back in a week for us to take another look at it," the consultant said.

"So I can definitely go home today?" I asked.

"Yeah," he said, like it was the most obvious thing in the world. I think I cheered, I was so happy. A huge flood of relief washed over me. It didn't matter how long it took – whether I'd be home in a few hours or had to wait until the evening – I was going home that day. I went to the day room to make some phone calls, accidentally knocking my glass of water off the table as I did so. I called for the nurse.

"Sorry," I said. "I was so excited that I decided to throw my glass of water across the floor."

I decided that what probably happened was that a more junior doctor had looked at my blood test and wasn't sure if I could go home based on that, so he had wanted a more senior opinion to confirm whether I could go home. That day was exceptionally busy, and the weekend never helps with this at hospitals due to staff shortages, so there was nobody senior available to ask and they were all dealing with more urgent things. If they had been available they probably would have said that I could go, which is why the answer when the doctors came around in the morning was that yes, of course I could go, no problem. I wondered what the impact had been down in ICU though, as the nurses were fully expecting me to leave on the Friday, and they had already promised my bed to someone else coming up from that department.

Peter came when visiting hours started. I had eaten a little lunch and was feeling fairly good. It was a couple of hours after that when the nurse came with my discharge papers and medication. And then we were gone, once again armed with Fragmin so that I could inject myself at home for a few weeks – this time in the stomach, which was helpfully completely numb in places.

It felt very strange to go. It was tiring just to walk to the car, and it certainly felt odd to get in the car and drive out of the hospital grounds. I had been in there for ten days and had barely seen any outside life. Not many of the windows on the ward had a view of anything except the rooftops of the neighbouring wings. It was November so it went dark while we were driving home, and the roads, as well as our flat when we got there, all felt unfamiliar to me. I had a tiny amount of dinner as in the early days I could barely manage anything. The trick was to eat little and often – around six small meals a day. The idea of three square meals went out of the window for quite a while. I also had a can of Coke and then spent the rest of the night wondering why I was in so much pain. Then I remembered from recovering from my previous operation – it was wind. I had been wondering why it hurt so much, and it took me hours to figure out that I had done it to myself. I had an antacid tablet and walked around the flat for a while, trying to get my wind up. There had been a woman in the same ward as me

129

who had suddenly suffered from bad pain and didn't know why. That was gas, too. I should have known, for her and for me. I was supposed to be experienced in this – I was a seasoned patient and should have remembered how painful wind can be. I was a little disappointed for both of us that we hadn't had anything in the way of explanation about what life would be like after surgery – what pains to expect, what not to eat and drink, and so on. I didn't get much sleep that night, but at least I was back in my own bed and knew to stay off Coke for a while.

Chapter Eight
Recovering From Whipple Surgery

Recovering from Whipple surgery was even worse than recovering from the hysterectomy. My day would consist of getting out of bed, curling up on the armchair in the best position I could manage, watching TV, eating a tiny amount of food, and going back to bed in the evening. That was it. For weeks I didn't even pick up my laptop, which was unlike me. I had similar problems to when I'd had my hysterectomy – wind pain, acid reflux, and a new symptom – painful spots on my tongue which may have been oral thrush, and made it even harder for me to eat. I couldn't drive so Peter took my car out at the weekends to keep the battery ticking over. My parents visited me, and when Peter went back to work I got up at 7am so that he could take me to their house on his way to work and pick me up on the way home.

Jess, whose messages I had accidentally ignored while I was in the HDU, came to visit me, bringing a lovely book for me to read and some chocolate. Little chocolate yule logs – a small piece of Christmas I could enjoy. Chris visited, too – though during this time I felt of very little company to anyone. He reassured me that I didn't need to be, that people just wanted to see me. I was desperate to be more present than I was, and felt like I was neglecting a variety of friendships, but there wasn't much I could do about it except wait until I felt better.

A week after my surgery, Peter and I went back to Leicester to have my drain reviewed. I was hoping that it could be removed, but no such luck – there was still a lot of fluid coming out of it, so I would be quite ill if they let all of that go into my stomach instead. For the next few weeks, we would have to continue the unpleasant and rather smelly task of emptying the drain and measuring the fluid that came out of it. It took me back to my days of having a colostomy bag. I was disappointed because the drain was beginning to get a bit uncomfortable, and stabbed me slightly if I leant on my side the wrong way. I wanted to feel normal again, and that wasn't going to happen until I could get the drain out.

A week before my birthday in December we ended up at the out of hours GP because my wound was infected. I had been worried about it on the Thursday because I thought the skin around part of the wound looked a little red. The wound itself had been weeping yellow-green pus, but I figured that was normal because my hysterectomy wound had done the same thing. On Friday morning I considered going to the GP but the wound looked the same as it did the day before, so I didn't bother. In the evening I wished I did because when Peter and I got home I checked the wound and it had a funny yellowish bulge that hadn't been there in the morning. It just wasn't healing at all and didn't look right. Annoyingly, by the time I realised this, it was nearly 6pm and the only thing we could do was call 111 at six-thirty to get some advice. I called up and they asked me some questions about the wound, none of which seemed relevant to my situation. Was it bleeding? No. It was leaking pus and looking red around the edges, but they didn't ask about any of that. The woman I spoke to said that someone from the out of hours surgery would be in touch with me to arrange an appointment within the next six hours. We had dinner and I spent the next couple of hours waiting for the phone to ring.

At about twenty past eight I got a phone call offering me an appointment. I could either go to Northampton at quarter to ten, or I could go to Kettering at 9pm. I took the second option and we made it there right on time. I saw the doctor and he confirmed that it was infected, and took a swab sample of the gunk. He said I should take it easy and not do anything to aggravate it. Peter and I both had colds and it might have been my coughing that had made it split open a bit. The doctor prescribed me antibiotics – ones I had taken before for my abscess and had gotten along with, though they had made me a bit hungry – and we picked them up on the way home. I had to call the GP a few days later to get the results of the swab, to make sure that I was on the correct antibiotics. I was. But I hated the feeling of being responsible for what happened to my body. I wanted to get better and that meant building up my strength by getting up and about, but I didn't want to upset my wound any further. I was already sitting around and napping during the day, so I wasn't sure how much easier I could take it.

The following weekend was my birthday, and I had asked my sister if we could have a gathering at her house. Her house was lovely and big, and her husband Neil was a great cook. He always put on a huge spread and encouraged everyone to get drunk. I wouldn't be getting drunk this time, but I had been looking forward to eating lots of good food and having a nice time with my friends and family. I love having a birthday near Christmas because it makes it feel that extra bit festive.

The day of my party came and though I had just finished the antibiotics, the wound still seemed infected and I didn't feel as good as I had hoped I would. Back when I was about to have my surgery, my birthday and Christmas seemed so far away. I even asked Mr Bhardwaj if I'd be having Christmas dinner and he said yes, of course I would. But these events had suddenly crept up on me and I didn't feel up to celebrating at all. I was worried that Christmas and all of the festivities leading up to it were passing me by.

It was mid-afternoon on Saturday and I'd been having a nap. Peter was in the bedroom and I was in the armchair in the living room. I woke up and went to the toilet, then came back in and sat down again. I could feel something wet on my belly. I lifted up the thick square of dressing that I usually tucked into my underwear to keep it covering the part of the wound that was leaking. The whole dressing was covered in yellow-green gook. It looked like the yellow, bulging bit of the wound had gotten bigger and ultimately exploded everywhere. I yelled for Peter to come in, and he took a look at it. We got me cleaned up with a new dressing, but the thing was still leaking. We had to decide whether or not I would be going to my own birthday party. I really wanted to go, though car rides were still painful and I knew I should have been resting. After going back and forth about it, I finally decided that we were going. We brought plenty of dressings with us so that I could change them if things got messy. It turned out to be a good night. We had chicken fajitas and I managed more than I usually did. My appetite was continuing to grow. I was sitting on the couch for the whole evening but I was still very uncomfortable. We had birthday cake and Neil hosted a quiz, but by ten-thirty, I was tired and needed to go home. I'd never left a family gathering so early, but I was out of energy. We said our thanks and left. A couple of weeks after the event, around Christmas, I would be told how much better I looked than I did on my birthday — apparently, I had been looking pretty worse for wear. I had barely noticed, myself. I think I had been somewhat pre-occupied with finding a dress I could wear that would be baggy enough to hide my swollen tummy and the drain that was still sticking out of it.

The following week was my work Christmas meal — another event I was absolutely determined to go to. Usually, I would get happily drunk and we'd be one of the last couples there. But this time I was ready to go soon after dessert. It was great to see everyone though, and they all seemed happy to see me. It was particularly nice to hang out with people from work and have no actual work to think about. By that time I had been away for three months and I had to keep reminding myself that I wasn't retired and that eventually, I would be going back. Nicola asked how I was getting on and I commented that the good thing about the second surgery was that it was really helping me to forget about the first surgery.

This was completely true — my time in hospital for the hysterectomy felt like hardly any problem at all compared to my ten-day stay for the Whipple. But the idea of not having any children did get to me a little. I saw photos of my Facebook friends with their kids and it made me feel happy and sad at the same time. I deactivated my Facebook for a while because I didn't want to see photos of people I didn't really care about and their babies. If I saw any adverts on social media for products or articles about pregnancy or parenting, I would click that I didn't want to see this type of advert, and marked it as not relevant to me. It felt good to have a little control over that.

I slowly started to recover from the Whipple surgery. I went from being hardly hungry at all to being hungry constantly, especially while I was on the antibiotics. I would go to my parents' house and have a cereal bar when I got there, followed by toast an hour or two later. Then a small sandwich for lunch, and perhaps a snack in the afternoon. Then I'd go home and have a small portion of whatever we were having for dinner. Over time I began to be able to eat more in one sitting, and a couple of months after the surgery I was back to eating regular portions.

I was still in pain because all I had in the way of pain relief was paracetamol. When Mary's brother Paul saw me at the pub quiz again for the first time since my Whipple surgery, he asked what pain medication I was on.

"Just paracetamol."

"So nothing, then? Paracetamol might as well be nothing."

"Yeah, pretty much!" I grinned. I was hardcore. But really, it had surprised me how painful recovering from the surgery was, despite the warnings I had received from my key worker. I had always thought of surgery as an easier option compared to chemotherapy and radiation. I thought I didn't have it as bad as other people because I was only having surgery. I don't think that way anymore. It was difficult to keep dismissing my experience as no big deal when I couldn't even pick up something myself if I'd dropped it on the floor. Even getting dressed every day was a mission, so most days I was too exhausted to bother if I didn't need to.

One day in December I received a letter that instilled panic in me all over again. It was a letter sent from Dr Das to an oncologist at Northampton Hospital. In it, he thanked her for agreeing to see me to talk about adjuvant chemotherapy. The letter said that there wasn't much evidence about whether or not chemo would help someone in my situation but that it was worth a discussion. Well, what a way for me to hear that I might have to have chemo – in a letter that wasn't even addressed to me. It was like eavesdropping on a conversation you didn't want to hear, in paper form. I had to look up the word adjuvant and understood from the internet that adjuvant chemotherapy is chemo you might have after surgery, not necessarily to get rid of the cancer, which I hoped had already gone, but to prevent it from returning.

I was due to see Mr Bhardwaj for a follow-up appointment a couple of weeks before Christmas, so I decided to bring it up with him. He apologised for the way I had found out about the chemo, even though it wasn't anything to do with him. I was just happy that someone had acknowledged that the letter wasn't the best way for me to find out about it, and I resigned myself to going to the appointment with the oncologist. Mr Bhardwaj confirmed that they had gotten rid of the cancer with clear margins and that it hadn't spread to the lymph nodes. I said that I thought clear margins meant that it was definitely all gone and no chemo was needed. He said that for pancreatic cancer and duodenal cancer, it was becoming more common for patients to go through chemo as well as surgery, as a preventative step. The nurse took the drain out for me that day, which was a relief after having it in for about six weeks. However, Mr Bhardwaj recommended that I keep a bag over the drain to catch any fluid or gunk that might come out of it, just for a few days. So it was like having a colostomy bag again. Mr Bhardwaj took the flange off my drain, and the dressing that I had put on the drain site next to it came along with it as it was all stuck together. Then the nurse came along and put the new flange on top of the site of the now-removed drain –without putting a new dressing on the other drain site (perhaps not realising that there was ever one there, despite it not being healed at all yet). So that drain site had the sticky part of the flange placed directly on top of it, which I wouldn't realise until I got home. The next day, I would lie on my bed at my parents' house after my shower while my mother attempted to gently pull flange glue off the top of my drain site – which is basically a small wound in the belly that is left to heal on its own after having a little plastic pipe sticking out of it.

Mr Bhardwaj discharged me back to Dr Das, which meant I might have never needed to set foot in Leicester General Hospital ever again. I very much hoped that was the case. Christmas came around and the day itself was easier than the run-up to it. Not being able to drive myself anywhere or walk around much meant I didn't get to soak up the atmosphere like I usually would, and my enjoyment of the season was somewhat limited to television adverts and movies, and attempting to wrap presents while sitting in my armchair and trying not to exhaust myself. Mr Bhardwaj had said I would be eating

Christmas dinner with my family like usual and I did –
just a smaller portion. Peter took me to my parents'
house in the morning where we exchanged presents,
then we went to Karen and Neil's house for dinner and
stayed into the evening, at which point Peter came back
from seeing his family and took me home. In all of this,
it did feel very good for Peter and the rest of my family
to be spending time together – this time luckily it was a
social event rather than an eight-hour wait for me to get
out of surgery.

The appointment with the oncologist was set up
for early January. Northampton General Hospital was
kitted out with a refurbished chemotherapy suite and
was the best hospital in the area to go to for this. We sat
in the waiting room watching Jeremy Kyle with the
other patients. I looked around and wondered how many
of them were having chemo and who was there for other
treatments or consultations. It was perhaps the best
waiting room I had been in, if we are indeed now rating
waiting rooms. It was warm and welcoming and had its
own café.

The appointment with the oncologist was long
and very informative. Dr Gabitass said that the
duodenum is so small that it's rare to get cancer in that
particular place, which is why there isn't much evidence
at the moment as to whether or not chemo will help keep
the cancer away. She said we should apply the logic of
bowel cancer to the situation - i.e., what would we do if
it were bowel cancer instead? She went through the list
of characteristics of the cancer that would mean that I
should have chemo, and none of those characteristics
applied to my situation. The only real reason we were
having the conversation at all was because of my age.

And strangely, the fact that I had Lynch syndrome meant that she felt less inclined to push me towards chemo because there was no evidence that cancer caused by Lynch syndrome would be helped with chemo in this situation. If I did have the chemo, it would be in tablet form instead of IV, because the IV form has more side effects. I would be on tablets for 14 days and then take a break for a week, and this would go on for six months. Six months sounded like an awfully long time. Add to that, the main side effect was diarrhoea, and if that happened I wouldn't be able to tell if it was because of the chemo or if it was just my internal pouch having an off day. The tablets also mean a patient has to have a certain enzyme for them to work properly, and two per cent of people don't have the enzyme. When this is the case, the body can't get the chemo out of its system, so it's like being on chemo forever. There is a test you can take to find out if you have the enzyme before treatment starts, but it isn't available on the NHS.

Everything was stacking up against me saying yes to chemo. I knew that if I said no to treatment and the cancer did come back I would be kicking myself for not doing it. But it could come back either way and I would never know if chemo made a difference or not. I had been under surveillance for eight years and that had kept me safe so far, so I thought I would continue to rely on that. I didn't want my life to be on hold for another six months. I wanted to go on holiday. I wanted to go back to work like everyone else and feel normal. As there wasn't much evidence of chemo being beneficial to someone like me, I already knew what my answer was going to be before we even left the appointment. I called my key worker the following week to let her know I wouldn't be having chemo, and I looked forward to making plans for the future.

It wasn't until mid-January that I began driving again, finally getting my independence back. Peter went back to work a week into January, and I decided that I could quite happily be on my own during the day. After weeks of asking Peter and my parents to make my food and drink for me and take me places, at the start of 2019 I started to look after myself again. I was glad of it. I've always been independent and happy in my own company, so I liked to be fairly self-sufficient. I was happy to stay at home during the day and watch TV or write, depending on how productive I felt. I drove myself to work and had a meeting with my manager Lorna and Nicky from HR, both of whom were very supportive. We decided I'd start going back to work again part-time in February and build my hours back up to full-time. I also started up my literary magazines again in January, once I had decided that I wasn't going to have chemo and there was a chance life could properly begin again.

The time leading up to starting work again felt strange. I was emotional after both of my surgeries, and I was crying at everything. I even cried at a McDonald's advert in which a girl bought a boy an ice cream. I was also in a sort of no man's land, wondering what I was supposed to be doing. My parents and I decided to do something spontaneous. We wanted to see the Northern Lights, so we spent four nights in Iceland. Unfortunately, the lights weren't so keen on coming out to play, and although we did see a bit of a white streak, we decided someone must have been playing with the dimmer switch that night. It was a little disappointing to be out on a boat in the cold sea for three hours and not see much of a show, but during our trip we also went on the Golden Circle tour and saw the geysers and the waterfalls, and met some Icelandic horses. (One of them bit me on the arm, but only gently, so I like to think it was because he wanted to play and not because he hated me.) Coming home to one degree above freezing felt positively toasty after we had been wandering around Reykjavik in minus twelve the day before.

Iceland

I see the fire before I see
the land of ice, I see sun-dipped
clouds as I soar and they are
on fire until they become field,
they are pink and they look like
solid ground, like the future
often does —
curiously comforting,
suspiciously static
the above and the below soften
so much they begin to merge,
above the below I see it clearly.

I hold the fire,
I am the fire, at least
that's what I tell myself
the future is soft fire burning
only to help, to warm, not to
scald or char. Perhaps all fire
thinks it is helping, I muse

as the plane begins to droop

my eyes are starry-skied
and we land, we drink in
the landscape, we settle in,
we drink blue lagoons with
lemon moons
carved out by a careful
barman's hands, I sit back
in a chair too big for me,
I watch the snow through the
draughty window and fear
the pavement, hope my shoes
grip like a needle knowing its
place on vinyl. Something about
this place feels final, this is a
once-only place, a one-shot place
the land of fire and I see it all,
the frozen waterfalls caught in the
act, geysers performing on command,
tales of elves that might just be true

we climb high to get the best view
of even higher places, we go down
into the basement to look at
volcano photography but I feel
nothing is on top of me, I feel
we could slide through this entire
city, I feel broken but patched up
with parts that are new, I feel
like maybe this is a ritual:
travel is not just a place you go
but a place that goes to you.

Before I went back to work, I would have an appointment with Mr Rashed to talk about what annual tests he was now going to send me for, and an appointment with Miss Biswas to decide whether I should go on HRT for menopause symptoms. If I didn't, I would have to have regular bone scans to check for signs of osteoporosis. I was doing okay during that time but I always got nervous before appointments. And my hair was falling out. It had been doing it for two or three weeks, now – large amounts coming out when I combed my hair, when I had a shower, or even just when I ran my fingers through it. I put it down to stress because it had happened to me before – when I was fifteen and my grandparents died. Hair can start falling out around three months after the stressful thing, and I had many stressful things to attribute it to. I was getting annoyed with pulling the hair out of my blanket, off my clothes, off my wet hands in the shower. It was just a cosmetic problem, and nothing to be worried about – just annoying and a little upsetting at times. If it was all going to fall out, I wished it would just get on with it already so that I could make peace with it and learn how to tie a headscarf.

The week before I went back to work in February, I had two appointments. The first was on Thursday with Mr Rashed, and the second was the next day with Miss Biswas in gynaecology. Sound familiar? The symmetry of life is funny. Absolutely hysterical. In the back of my mind, I worried that it was the same thing happening again – bad news from one, and then bad news from the other the very next day. Really, I knew that they couldn't give me much in the way of bad news because I wasn't awaiting any results for anything. Mr Rashed asked me how my Whipple procedure went and how I had been doing. He said he was going to leave me alone for a while, but I prodded him.

"So no CT scans or anything?"

"When was your last one?"

"I had one while I was in hospital in November."

"Well, we can't do another one until six months after that date. So I'll send you for one in May."

"What about the sigmoidoscopy you usually send me for?"

"When was your last one?"

"April last year."

"That's been nearly a year then, so I'll send you for one of those."

I didn't want to go for a CT scan or a sigmoidoscopy (though they are the lesser of the evil tests). I would have very much liked to have been left alone. But I didn't want to be deserted. I still wanted to be looked after and monitored. What if it came back and we didn't notice because I wasn't having enough surveillance? I didn't think this was a time to be lax about these things. There is no time to be lax about these things. So I left the appointment fairly happy.

The appointment with Miss Biswas was mainly to talk about whether or not I should go on HRT to manage menopause symptoms. I sat in the waiting room among the pregnant women and babies. If you're wondering whether or not that's fun when you've recently had a hysterectomy – it's not. I was called in and we talked about HRT. The MDT had decided that I shouldn't go on it because it carried a small cancer risk due to the oestrogen. Sticking with the theme of not wanting to take any risks, I agreed that was fine. I was given a prescription for some medication for my bones and told I would be referred to an endocrinologist to set up some bone scans to look out for osteoporosis, which is a risk during the menopause. Miss Biswas also said she was going to give me a quick exam, so she and the nurse left the room while I took off my bottom half of clothes and laid down on the bed. I waited a couple of minutes, then heard about five women say "Awwww!" all at the same time. There was a baby in the corridor behind the consultation room, where Miss Biswas and the nurse had just disappeared. I sat listening to the chatter of the women and the baby's gurgling and crying. It was another five minutes or so before they finally reappeared to examine me. Of course, I understood their preference to coo over a baby rather than to examine the insides of an infertile, menopausal woman. Which is exactly what I felt like I was at that precise moment.

Part Two
The Small Intestine

Chapter Nine
What's So Traumatic About Cancer?

Life After Cancer: Expectation vs. Reality

Life after cancer was very different from what I had expected. This book is laid out in a similar way to how I have experienced cancer: action first, thoughts and feelings later. There isn't much time to think about it when you're going through it all. It's not until treatment is over and you're expected to go back to normal life, that the stress starts to show. When everything calms down, when you're looking and feeling better, when you're going back to work and to everyday life, when you and everyone else has stopped talking about it – I found that was when I started thinking about it the most. It takes a while for your brain to catch up with everything that has happened. Back in 2010, hearing that the cancer was gone and that I didn't need chemo didn't send me soaring out into a carefree world. In fact, I was haunted by everything that had happened to me. When you really think about it, the idea that we would switch from being worried and stressed to suddenly being happy and feeling like everything is normal again is unrealistic. And if it does happen that way, there are likely some unresolved feelings there that are going to rise up again eventually, even if you are celebrating at first.

When people talk about trauma, they are often talking about childhood abuse, sexual assault, soldiers at war, and so on. Cancer and other illnesses generally don't get a look in. In fact, if you research the subject online you're more likely to find articles talking about the physical effects of mental stress, and how stress may contribute to causing some illnesses, including cancer. But fewer people are talking about it when the subject is flipped around. What about the effect physical illness can have on a person's mental health? (Add to that, what about the fact that the stress of having an illness can have its own physical effects on the body?) Everyone wants to "raise awareness" of cancer (though I think we are all very much aware of its existence by now), but there isn't much conversation going on about the emotional and mental health problems that can arise from having the disease.

So what's so bothersome about cancer? I've had tests, surgery, and more tests to see if it's still there or come back. Well, now it's gone. I don't have cancer anymore. I don't need any more operations or nasty treatment. It's all in the past – it's time to just get over it and move on with my life already! That's what I should be saying, right?

But there is so much wrong with all of that I hardly know where to begin. Before I had cancer, I had no idea how much this stuff stays with you. There's the physical stuff like colostomy bags, weight loss, hoping I don't put too much back on, tiredness and the amount of time it takes to feel fully recovered from surgery, little twinges of pain from surgical sites when I move the wrong way or sneeze, hair loss, and of course scars. And then there are the emotional effects, like sadness, grief, fear of recurrence, anxiety, anger, self-pity – the list goes on. Not pretty feelings. That's not even touching on the physical and emotional effects of the menopause, which for me has been mainly hot flushes so far. And the effects of having a hysterectomy and coming to terms with never having biological children. Sadness for yourself, guilt for not being able to give your partner something they want, jealousy towards women who are pregnant or who have children. And all that coming from someone who was never desperate to have children to begin with, so it must be so much worse for someone who had their heart set on being a mother.

Knowing all that, it's easy to see that "moving on" from cancer is not simple. I'm going to take each idea people may have about cancer survivorship – some of the things we might think and expect from ourselves or that we may hear from others, in society or in the media – and deconstruct them.

"Your cancer has gone."

I can't say "yes, my cancer has gone" without adding "as far as I know" straight after. It could come back at any time, and I wouldn't know unless my next round of check-ups picked it up. Fear of recurrence is a reality for many cancer survivors, and for good reason. It's a completely normal and natural worry, but that doesn't make living with it any easier. And I know it sounds like I'm not grateful for it being gone and I'm not "living my best life", but I am grateful and happy that it's gone. It's just that survivorship isn't all climbing mountains and giving back to charities or ditching your job to follow your dreams because you've suddenly realised how short life is and that you have to make every second count. I did realise that after my first surgery – hence the hot air balloon ride and firewalk and trip to New York. There are days, or sometimes just minutes, when I feel great about having come through the other side of whatever recent treatment or diagnosis I have had. But I'm still worried that I might have to go through it all over again.

"It's all in the past."

It is all in the past, but that means it happened. It's not like I dreamt it (although sometimes it might feel like I did). This is a thing that took place, and saying it's all behind us doesn't make it all magically go away. And I know another thing people might say is "don't let it define you". But I do, and I will continue to do so. I've had cancer three times, and I have a genetic condition that means I might get it again. There is no rule book for learning how to live with these things. And like some cancer survivors, I may sometimes feel like I am doing survivorship "wrong". Not taking on some big personal challenge for charity (wasn't cancer enough of a challenge on its own?), or not being "brave" and smiling through the whole thing, or not simply forgetting about everything that happened as if there were no chance of it ever happening again. There is no right or wrong way to "do" cancer, and that includes how much you let it define you. I mean, if it's the only thing you think about and the rest of your life, interests and personality have fallen by the wayside and been replaced only by your "survivor" label, then that could be a problem. And some people don't like the survivor label. Similarly, I don't like the war language – "he lost his battle", "she's fighting cancer" –as far as I'm concerned, nobody is winning, and the word "fight" makes it sound like it's our responsibility to rid ourselves of the disease. As if the people who lost their battle weren't trying hard enough. But I digress. Some of us want to forget it ever happened, and that's okay. Some of us want to reframe it into something we feel proud of for "beating" (don't like that word, either). And some of us feel like it is one part of us that will never go away. And this is fine, too. Do whatever you need to do. Write about it. Talk about it. Use it to spur you on to do great things. Put it in your spare bedroom, lock the door and pretend it isn't there. It's all good. But don't discount your past or anyone else's like what happened was no big deal. That seems dismissive. It was a big deal. Whether you choose to think of it as still a big deal now is up to you.

Cancer survivors might want to use their experience to help support other people going through treatment. Or use it to become an advocate, a charity ambassador, or write about it in their memoirs. Or they might want to forget about it and try to move on. There is no right way or wrong way to do cancer. We're all navigating blindly, trying to make the right decisions for ourselves. Whatever we choose is the right decision for us.

"You don't need any more treatment."

Maybe I'm being left alone in terms of treatment for now, but I still have to go for appointments with my consultants. I still need regular check-ups. The threat is still there. And it's hard to deal with that and get on with your normal life. Imagine that you have gone back to work, but halfway through your day you get a phone call inviting you to come to a CT scan next week. You have to excuse yourself from your colleagues to take the call. Then figure out how you are going to arrange the appointment around your work hours. Then lose concentration at work in the days or hours before your scan, depending on how worried you are about this particular appointment. Try to put it to the back of your mind because you have to focus on other things. Look around you at everyone else for whom this is just a normal day. You might forget about it for a while, distracted by normal life. But then you'll suddenly remember, and have that feeling of dread again. Maybe your stomach will flip. A bit like when you wake up in the morning and just for a few seconds you have no idea what your world is like, and everything is at peace. Then you wake up properly and remember – *oh yes, I have an appointment*, or *I have cancer*, or *I'm scared*. Whatever it is, wherever you are in your experience, it's like hearing the news or picking up the phone or reading the letter all over again. Maybe treatment is over, maybe the cancer is gone. But the worrying might not be.

"It's time to get over it and move on with your life."

I can't get over something that is still happening. Yes, there is moving on in some form, in our own time. But we will get over it in our own way when we are ready. Plus, if you never look back at the past, how are you supposed to learn from it? It's all very well forgetting the whole thing happened, but not to the point of not being vigilant with new symptoms, or not pushing to get the check-ups you need. Sometimes my consultant doesn't mention sending me for check-ups without me prodding a little, so there is some responsibility there. The past keeps me on my toes, which, while an uncomfortable position to be in, is important for my overall wellbeing.

The Trauma of Living with a Changed Body

I have mixed feelings about my body. I don't mind my scars – I think scars are actually pretty cool. If I feel like my belly isn't sticking out too much, I occasionally even wear tops that show off my midriff. I'm almost proud of my scars. But that's about the only positive thing I have to say about my post-cancer body. My belly is a weird shape due to having various organs removed (though it is quite cool to be able to put my hands on my waist and feel where my latest removed organs should be). My scars are fine once they are scars, but for months after surgery, I couldn't look at myself in the mirror without freaking out. Between the wound, my drain sites which were still covered over with dressings after my Whipple, and my stomach, which was swollen straight after surgery and didn't look that much better afterwards, my belly was a mess. I remember when I was much younger and had a flat stomach – I was always a skinny kid. My body looks different now and it's like part of my identity has changed. Add to that, after the hysterectomy I was in the menopause, having hot flushes and the odd freak-out about whether my ankles might be swollen. And I couldn't have children. I couldn't do the thing I should be able to do as a woman. I had lost not only my colon, my duodenum, my womb, but all of the collateral damage that was removed at the same times – those "just in case" or "might as well" or "this is the only way" organs – the head of my pancreas, my ovaries, gallbladder, bile duct, appendix, cervix. Fallopian tubes, I think. I'm not even certain anymore. But my hysterectomy made me feel like less of a woman. I would look at pregnant women who were cool and glowing and purposeful, and I was a menopausal hot mess, sweaty and empty. Hollow and pointless. What a way for a person to think of themselves.

At the beginning of 2019, I felt old before my time. I had been through too much, and I had seen too much. How can a person get over the trauma of illness when there are so many glaring reminders of the past right in front of their eyes?

The Burden of Responsibility

Having cancer the first time made me feel very responsible for my own health. I thought that if it came back and it was advanced when they found it, that it would be my fault for not being vigilant enough. I know about cancer and I know I can get it because I've had it before, so I should be on the lookout for it now and be able to help my medical team catch it early. If I die from cancer, it's my fault. But the cancer did come back, and I needed two surgeries. Luckily they were both early stage. And I didn't feel guilty like I thought I might. I know it isn't my fault. Even though without Mr Doshi, my uterine cancer wouldn't have been caught, and in that case, I should have been more vigilant. Perhaps if I had said no to the hysteroscopy and then found out later that it was cancer and it was advanced, then I might feel guilty or responsible. But that would be a different story and thank goodness that isn't what happened.

Fear of the Unknown

The thought of something happening inside my body that I know nothing about is very scary. Anything could be happening in there and I wouldn't know because I didn't know the first time. When I think about the fact that I have Lynch syndrome, it's sometimes difficult not to freak out. Lynch syndrome means you have a defective gene, and that gene is supposed to stop cancer from developing. When it doesn't work, cancer can carry on without interruption. And both of my genes are defective. So that's two things that are supposed to stop cancer if it rears its ugly head, and they don't. It's all I can do to not fly into a panic when I think about the fact that cancer could be growing right now, in my own body, and the things that are supposed to stop it are just sitting there broken, and I have no idea it's happening – and my body might not show me the signs until it's too late. Yes, I've been lucky so far when it comes to catching it. But will I be lucky for my whole life?

Grief

I feel like I have grieved more for myself than I have for anyone I have known who has died. But then, isn't all grief for the self, in some way? I wouldn't really know, but I can't help but think that there are some parallels between cancer and grief. Part of cancer *is* grief, in fact. Grieving for the life we thought we were going to have, but we've had to put on hold through treatment, and then once treatment is over it all looks different. Grief for the body we used to have, which now also looks different and we may have lost faith in. Grief for our previous state of ignorance about our own mortality. Grief for the peace of mind we have lost. Grief for lost friendships. Grief for fertility, or anything else we have lost. Grief for the things we thought were going to happen but were no longer a possibility. There are so many losses in cancer. With that comes inevitable grief.

Changed Perceptions

Cancer has also changed my perceptions. Yes, in some ways that has been a positive change – it has made me worry less about small things, be impulsive, try to get what I want more, be more grateful. It's made me grateful for every birthday because getting old is a privilege not everyone gets to enjoy. But it's influenced the way I see things. I remember walking past a tree with huge knobbly knots on its trunk and instead of seeing it simply for what it was, I saw a tree that looked like it had a tumour. It's gotten in my head like that, infiltrating everything, changing the way I see everything. No wonder I sometimes try to avoid reminders like cancer charity adverts, TV shows and movies with cancer-related storylines, and so on, if I can see cancer and feel alarmed just by looking at a tree.

It's Not All Trauma

That's right, cancer and illness is not all trauma and terror – there is boredom, too. Here are some mundane things I haven't mentioned so far, which were very present and though not traumatic in themselves, added to the worry and tedium of cancer:

- **Blood tests**. Because they happened so many times, and unlike cannulas when I was in hospital, blood tests were never a problem for me.
- **Waiting rooms**. Waiting rooms are not difficult to hate. I dread to think how many hours in total I have spent sitting in waiting rooms staring at empty chairs and listening to other peoples' names being called. I hate hearing my full name being said because it is usually only said in the context of a waiting room or by medical professionals.
- **Hospital food.** Boring, and pretty terrible, for the most part. In Leicester, everything was steamed. So even if fish fingers and chips sounded appealing, it was all soft and soggy. Best to go with pasta or something that isn't meant to be crunchy. As a side note, the cheese sandwiches were very nice. But when the medication rounds take place while you're eating lunch, and the trainee nurse stands over you to make sure you're taking your tablets, and you end up rushing eating what's in your mouth and immediately taking the tablet, and then pretty much immediately throwing up everything you've just eaten because of that, a cheese sandwich suddenly isn't quite so appealing.
- **Observations.** I know the nurses have to come around and do my blood pressure, and take my temperature and so on, and that's fine. But after ten days in hospital, the questions "have you been to the toilet?" and "have you had a bowel movement today?" start to wear thin. And the

observations about how much I was eating were a little upsetting. I'd just had Whipple surgery. I couldn't eat much. And I was having to explain myself whenever a nurse would come around and ask how much I'd had for lunch that day. I was eating as much as I could, and as much as I thought was appropriate for my body considering the state it was in. It made me think again about Katie, who had been in hospital for five weeks, and how aggravating it all must have been for her.

There is so much mundanity surrounding cancer – including, of course, the boredom of hospitals. For most of my stay after my hysterectomy and for most of the time after my Whipple, I lay in bed and didn't do anything. I just didn't have the energy to go on the internet, read a book or do puzzles. It makes me depressed just thinking about it. There was anxiety, then boredom and mundanity, and more anxiety. A terrible combination. Sometimes it's not trauma. Sometimes it's boredom, too.

Sometimes I feel like it isn't trauma at all. I know I used to think I had PTSD, or I thought it would be better if I did because it sounded better than the alternative - being unnecessarily afraid was better than having something real to panic about. But going to the counsellor made me realise that there's nothing wrong with my mental health. And that's not easy, either. To be so anxious about something and to feel so emotionally messed up but to know that there is nothing wrong with you, mentally at least. My therapist seemed to think there was nothing we could do about things like health anxiety - it is what it is. While it sounded good that there was nothing wrong, it was also frustrating that the anxiety was normal and something that I just have to live with.

But why should I? Live with it, that is. The way I feel when thinking about what has happened to me isn't nothing. Fear of recurrence is not nothing. The problem I have, standing outside the closed door of cancer world and staring out into the horizon of the "new normal", is being able to differentiate between good old "normal" anxiety which there might be no therapy for and something that is more problematic and could potentially be fixed.

Sometimes I don't know what makes me anxious or scared or sad. Sometimes it's obvious – something I've seen or heard or read has reminded me about my experience of cancer or made me question whether my cancer will come back, or I'll simply have an upcoming appointment to worry about. But sometimes I'll just be nervous and I won't know what's triggered it. When I think back to the time between my first diagnosis and the next two, I remember feeling weirdly sad for no real reason at all. It is a very difficult thing to explain, but it feels like being in a particular place. Somewhere dark, and there is nobody else around, but that's okay. I am familiar with it and even comfortable in it. I wallow in it for a little while, until I eventually come out of it. Maybe it is me thinking about the past because feeling sad about what has already happened is better than feeling scared of what could happen in the future.

And now, months after my Whipple surgery, I feel rather confused. I thought I knew what to expect after cancer because I'd gone through it all already after my bowel surgery. I was supposed to feel sad and weird and in a dark place, but instead, Peter was telling me that I seemed much happier and he was glad. Ordinarily, that isn't something to complain about, and forgive me for moaning about feeling too happy, but I didn't expect it to be this way. Have I emotionally shut down temporarily? Or could it be that I am so used to cancer now, that the aftermath simply isn't bothering me this time around? Am I that much of a seasoned expert?

More likely, it's just early days. These things can take a while to ramp up and creep up on you when you least expect it. But how much of a strange person am I to almost *want* to feel sad? I want to get my emotional mileage out of this thing. Or maybe I just want a bit of control and part of that is in knowing what to expect, or thinking I do – and then when that expected thing doesn't turn up, the feeling of not having control returns, and the situation feels a bit more alien than it should.

Living in Two Worlds

I feel like part of the problem of dealing with cancer, and all the appointments and the anxiety, is the fact that I haven't united one world with another. There is the cancer world that I've been in for several months, and there is the world I left behind somewhat and have to return to – except it isn't the same, because I'm not the same. Putting the two worlds together could be a way to make peace with the cancer world. Maybe by merging it with my normal world, I would be making it smaller, but I'm worried that it would actually make my normal world smaller and the cancer world more significant. Part of the problem with doing this merging act could also be the fact that I can't talk to everyone in my world about the other world, and it's as if I have to pretend it doesn't exist. Or maybe I don't want the cancer world to exist so I pretend it isn't there. Maybe the trick is to not separate the worlds in my head but to accept both of them as part of my life.

The reality is, cancer is a lonely place to be – even if you have a great support network like I do. Friends and family might listen and come to appointments and help you out, but you're the only one this disease is actually happening to. And trying to live in one world and then the other makes it even more difficult.

The separation of two worlds is what makes it even more anxiety-inducing when one intrudes upon the other. For example, when I'm sitting at my desk at work and I get a call on my mobile from a withheld number. It's the hospital calling to arrange an appointment or something similar, and it causes immediate panic and stress, even if it's an appointment I've been expecting. When I know I have an appointment coming up but it hasn't been booked in yet, it doesn't feel quite real enough to be scary. But then I get a phone call or a letter and suddenly it's real and I have to think about it, take time off work, schedule it into my life. It pushes its way into my crowded brain and makes room for itself. And then it's like I'm not my normal self anymore, who I was trying to get back to, or was maybe even beginning to feel like again. It's a sudden regression, like being pulled backwards into a room you were trying to leave. There is no leaving.

Reality Check

It's time to stop for a reality check. Because I just stopped for five minutes to have a peek at Twitter, and I read a blog post written by someone who has stage four secondary breast cancer and has been told that she has an extra ten months to live. And that she should apparently feel lucky about it. She should be grateful for the fact that, at the age of 34, while all her friends are getting married and having babies, she has ten months of her life left to live. And here I am not dying at all, and complaining about how difficult it is for me to be alive.

I stand by it, though. Yes, I am very grateful that my situation is so much better than other people's. But someone else being in a worse position than you doesn't mean that you should be happy all the time and stop moaning. It doesn't mean your experience is nothing compared to theirs. Someone else's feelings don't negate yours or make it any better. Your experience and feelings are valid, and you have every right to talk about it, work through it and make the best out of whatever you have. Yes, be grateful that things aren't worse. But also know that your feelings are worth expressing, too. Cancer is horrendous for everybody. We're all facing something we once happily ignored: our own mortality.

Positives of Cancer

I'm not going to start professing about how cancer is a gift we should be grateful for. But there are a few positives to take away from my cancer experience. For example, I don't have periods anymore. My periods were super heavy and painful, to the point where I sometimes had to take days off work because of stomach cramps, and I took medication to try to make them lighter. So not curling up in a ball for five days every month is something I'm very happy about. Plus, I no longer have to worry about my periods coming while I'm on holiday or want to go for a swim (if I was going on holiday, you could guarantee that I would be on my period for at least part of it). Would I have rather kept my womb and my periods so that I could have children? Yes, I would. But I have to make do with what I've got, and we do have other options for having kids. One other thing to consider is that my biological children would inherit my faulty genes, so in my family at least, Lynch syndrome stops with me.

That's pretty much where the physical positives end. But there are mental upsides, too. I've already talked about all the things I decided I would do, which, without a prod from cancer, I might have left on my "one day" shelf. After my first diagnosis, I decided that "one day" wasn't good enough, because it might never come. I had more of a sense of urgency: it was time to get on with the things I really wanted to do. Another upside was that I made more of a point of being grateful for all the things I had, and to worry less about small things that might have bothered me before. I was even more laid back than I had been in the past – if that was possible.

And sometimes there is even cause for celebration. On the anniversary of the day I had my bowel removed, I make a mental note to feel grateful for being cancer-free for so long (or I did, before I got cancer elsewhere, anyway). "Cancerversaries" might be the day we find out we're cancer-free or the day of our diagnosis, and some people celebrate them and others don't. There's even a Cancer Survivor's Day on the first Sunday in June, which some people like but others don't, claiming that it disregards those who have died from cancer and those who are still going through treatment. It perhaps also sounds too triumphant and puts pressure on survivors to celebrate when it may be the last thing they feel like doing, considering the impact cancer has had on their quality of life.

So yes, there are things to be grateful for, but there is a lot of trauma surrounding cancer, too, and it shouldn't be ignored.

Chapter Ten
How Does Trauma Manifest Itself?

*It's a radiotherapy machine you have to work yourself –
yes, you, as the patient. A nurse is standing next to me
as I lie on the bed part of the machine. And I mean bed
in the loosest term possible – bed, as in something you
lie on, not anything providing comfort.*

*The nurse has short blonde, spiky hair and
glasses. She is wearing a small smile as if she doesn't
have a care in the world. I'm not sure what's happening,
but clearly, it isn't her job to tell me. Not her problem.*

*I have to point the laser part of the machine
myself. My hoodie keeps falling into its path and I pull it
out of the way. When the laser falls on a spot or blemish
– of which I appear to have several on my chest and
stomach – the display on the machine tells me whether
or not I should zap it. It tells me exactly what's wrong
with the spot and how likely it is that the laser will fix
the problem.*

*Press start to begin, the machine says. I don't
know if all this effort is going to make any difference. I
don't know if it will hurt. I think I'm supposed to hold
onto the handles above my head but I need at least one
hand free to work the machine. I press start and point
the laser at one of my bumpy red spots. It stings – not on
the surface, but deeper. I flit from one spot to another.
There are several of them. I don't know how long I should
point the laser at each one. I don't know what I'm doing
but it's all on me. It's my fault if it doesn't work.*

I wake up. Something tells me I should be grateful it was a dream. I should feel lucky.

My nightmares don't make me feel lucky.

The above is just one example of many bad dreams I've had over the years, and bad dreams are just one of the ways in which trauma manifests itself. According to the NHS[1], symptoms of PTSD include:

- Nightmares
- Flashbacks
- Repetitive and distressing images
- Physical reactions such as sweating, pain and shaking
- Negative thoughts about the event
- Avoidance of people or places that act as reminders of the trauma
- Emotional numbing
- Feeling on edge or irritable
- Difficulty concentrating
- Insomnia

I can tick off a few of those myself, and I'd add the previously discussed back pain and hair loss that can come from intense stress. Those may not be PTSD symptoms, but they are certainly my body's way of telling me that all is not well in my head. I've had difficulty concentrating. My hands have shaken. I have avoided charity events for the sake of not having to think about cancer. I've had negative thoughts by the

---

[1] NHS, "Symptoms - Post-traumatic stress disorder (PTSD)" https://www.nhs.uk/conditions/post-traumatic-stress-disorder-ptsd/symptoms/

bucketful. You've already read one of my nightmares. And intrusive memories have been a problem, too.

Intrusive Memories

It was one day several years after my bowel surgery when I nearly cried because someone at work was eating toast at work. The smell of toast reminded me of being in hospital, where they would come around and ask us what we wanted for breakfast and I'd have toast with strawberry jam. I can't stomach the thought of strawberry jam now just thinking about it. And the toast smell trigger didn't make much sense because I had eaten it at home plenty of times since being in hospital back then. Maybe it was because it was in a public or unexpected place. So I have gotten upset over toast. I have also gotten upset because of the continuous beeping sound a printer was making. It sounded like hospital machinery – perhaps like when my morphine machine would make noises for seemingly no reason. I wanted to go over there and smash the thing, but I just sat at my desk willing it to stop.

Triggers are things that set off an emotional reaction in someone because they remind them of something traumatic. They set off a memory or flashback to the event, transporting the person back as if it is happening all over again. A trigger might be the smell of toast, or a beeping sound, or the taste of banana, or a thousand other seemingly harmless things. And the way the trigger affects a person isn't always the same. It might lead to a panic attack or physical symptoms such as shaking or having trouble breathing or feeling anxious. They can last a few minutes or much longer. Anxiety, stress and trauma look different on everyone.

Another time at work, I faced a trigger but I actively tried not to let the bad memory ruin my day. One of my work colleagues had just had a baby, so birth, labour, c-sections and epidurals were the morning's topic. I sat listening while working (it's a small office, it's impossible not to listen), until the bit about the epidural, at which point I grabbed my headphones, went to YouTube and clicked on the first music video I saw. Which, usefully, was Slipknot, but anything would have worked to drown out what they were saying. Because when I had my colon removed, if you remember, I had an epidural. God, it hurt. It hurt so much I wondered why they didn't give me anything first so I wouldn't feel the epidural going in. I don't know what an epidural looks like, or really where it goes. I remember sitting up in the anaesthetic room, which was like a cupboard leading to Narnia, except in this Narnia they slice you open. I remember them undoing my gown at the back so I was only an inch or two from losing what little dignity I had left. I remember swinging my legs around and sitting on the side of the bed so that they could put it in. I remember it felt violent, like they had to push really hard to get it in. And it hurt. A lot. I don't think I cried, but remembering it is like remembering something that happened while I was drunk or drugged up, it was so surreal. I was terrified. I remember getting ready for bed on my first day back at home and realising that after a week I still had some sort of sticker stuck to my back. It feels like another life ago now. And all that came flooding back because of a couple of people in the office talking about having an epidural during labour. I put music on and blocked out the rest of their conversation, and I told myself to stop thinking about it and to write it up at lunchtime if I just wanted to get it out. So I did. I set aside some time to think about it and write about it, and then move on with the rest of my day.

Six months after my Whipple procedure, when I had been back at work full time and left to my own devices for a while, I had a small influx of check-ups in the space of a couple of months. It was around then that my brain decided to get on with the important work of remembering. Little flashes. Peter and I went for dinner at my parents' house one evening and when we came back home, walking through the living room door felt like I was coming back from Peter picking me up after I had spent the day being looked after at mum and dad's, back when I was recovering from surgery. At that moment I remembered how much energy it took just to get out of the car and walk inside, and how much more energy it would take to get my coat off and get changed. Looking at the armchair just reminded me of how I used to collapse into it (gently) and how it would take so long for me to conjure up the energy and willpower to get up to do whatever I needed to do, like go to the toilet or take a shower, or get dressed. All of that flashed in my mind for a second, then left its remains lingering in my brain after I looked away.

And that wasn't the only way memories came about – there were and still are flashes of memories from that time that return completely unprovoked. Sitting in the ward waiting to be taken down to surgery for my hysterectomy. Being in hospital, not being able to sleep or get comfortable, getting stuck in the shower. Talking on the phone in the day room on the day I was finally released from hospital after the Whipple. My brain was finally catching up with everything.

Reliving the Event

Equally unprovoked, sometimes I just think about what has happened and relive my time in hospital or at a particular appointment, for no real reason. It doesn't help and I'm not thinking about what else could have happened or how I could have changed anything. I'm literally just going over things again in my head, whether or not something has prompted me to do so. It's upsetting and pretty pointless. There is no processing this, really. Sometimes I catch myself doing it and actively try to turn my attention towards something else. But sometimes, if there is something else to worry about, it feels safer to think about all the things that have already happened rather than what might happen in the future. To relive feels better than to speculate.

Avoidance

One day in 2015, I answered the phone to a cancer charity who had been calling me every day for the last couple of weeks. I had been avoiding answering the phone, partly because I was worried about the conversation being a trigger for me. I finally answered it and the guy on the line asked me why I had previously donated to a similar charity, to which I replied "personal experience".

I was then pressed further – "someone close to you?"

"Myself."

"What kind of cancer did you have?"

I probably should have just said mind your own business or something, but I went along with the conversation. Then the guy started talking about his cousin who'd had cancer, and had suffered from a low immune system due to the treatment, and asked if I have that problem, too. I didn't think so. Apparently, it was really difficult because nobody could visit his cousin if they had even the sniffles. That does sound difficult and though I sympathised, I hadn't asked and I didn't want to know or talk about it. I had never had a charity call me and ask me those kinds of questions or tell me their own personal, unsolicited anecdotes. I was right to avoid them and probably should have continued to do so.

Race For Life was something else I eventually avoided. I did it for two or three years after my first diagnosis, but at some point, I decided it was too much for me. Registering, asking people to sponsor me, setting up a donation page, training, talking to friends about it – it all put the subject at the forefront of my mind regularly, and that led to general feelings of sadness and feeling alone about the whole thing. So like phone calls and adverts and other charity events, I learned to shy away from it for the sake of my own mental health. It was easier to ignore it all than to do something philanthropic.

Physical Symptoms

A phone call from the hospital inviting me to an appointment can often set my hands shaking. Plus, I carry all my tension in my back and shoulders, so having a bad back comes from being stressed out – usually about something health-related. And having trouble catching my breath is another way I can tell I'm anxious about something. These things might happen if I'm feeling anxious about an upcoming appointment or a recent diagnosis, or even if I'm upset about something that happened in the past. In fact, I think I know how it feels to be a cancer survivor better than I know what it feels like to have cancer. After all, mine were all caught early with few symptoms if any, and no pain caused by it. I know how it feels to have tests and treatment and to deal with it all emotionally, but cancer itself is something of a vague, almost distant concept for me in terms of what it feels like. The physical symptoms of stress have been more immediate.

Clearly, cancer is something that's still happening if it's affecting the body in this way. The question is, what can be done to help cancer survivors deal with it all?

Chapter Eleven
Is the World Equipped For Us?

It is amazing what the human body can handle. I have found that my body is far more resilient than I would have imagined. After my hysterectomy, I was worried about what effect even more surgery would have on me when I had my Whipple. But it turned out, I recovered very well and even though it took a few months, my body has bounced back. It really is incredible what our bodies can cope with.

Physical Accessibility

However, during my recovery, I realised that the world wasn't completely equipped for people who may be a little infirm like I was. My shower incident in the hospital was a good example of this – though to be fair to the staff, they did get an engineer to come and have a look at the shower door afterwards. I don't know what the outcome of that investigation was, but I hope that they agreed it wasn't great for people who had just had surgery. I was surprised that nobody had had a problem with it before I did.

Other examples were things I discovered shortly after my first surgery and rediscovered after my second and third. I found that some taps in public toilets needed some force to turn them on – they really needed a hard push down on them, and I struggled with that a little after my bowel surgery. Heavy doors were also a problem, and when getting up off the toilet, I could really use something to pull myself up with – usually the toilet roll holder would have to do. A lack of chairs in some public places was also a problem, as were heavy chairs that are difficult to move. And since I had trouble bending down after my surgeries, I struggled with fitting rooms in clothes shops. If there was no bench or stool in the changing room, I had to put my things on the floor and bend down to pick them up. Or I struggled to put my shoes on if there was nowhere for me to sit down and tie my laces. It might sound like a small thing to complain about, but it was one of those things that made life a little more difficult. And looking around at the other changing rooms in the particular shop I have in mind, all of which looked quite small, it made me wonder how other people with disabilities manage when they have to deal with these kinds of problems all the time.

Support For Cancer Survivors

It's not just the physical things that make me wonder whether the world is really survivor-friendly. I continue to be surprised about how little the emotional and mental effects of cancer are spoken about. When I had my first surgery back in 2010, I wasn't directed to any resource where I could get support for the emotional side of things. It isn't a surgeon's job to provide this kind of support, but I think there should be more emphasis on the emotional and mental effects of cancer and surgery. Patients should be made aware that they might need support after treatment finishes. It may be harder to look for this kind of help when treatment is over because we're not seeing our medical team as regularly anymore (maybe not even at all), and people may not know where to go to talk to someone about this.

The few online articles written on the subject feature headlines such as "Cancer Survivors More Likely to Have Mental Distress Than Healthy Individuals"[2]. To some, this may seem like an innocuous headline, but for me, it is such an obvious statement that it provokes an exasperated eye-roll. Well of *course* we're likely to have mental distress. We've been told we have a serious illness, we've gone through horrible treatment for it, and even though it's now gone we're still worried that one day it might come back and we'll have to go through it all over again – or worse, it will kill us. It is good that these kinds of articles are being written and these issues are being talked about, but I'd like to get to a place where the statement "Cancer survivorship is emotionally challenging and can lead to mental distress" is as obvious a thing to say as "Cancer can kill people". Then maybe we'd have more in-depth conversations about what we can do about it.

So, what can we do about it? To find that out, we first need to know what cancer survivors need.

What Do Cancer Survivors Need?

I can't speak for everyone, but I can tell you what I need, regardless of whether these needs are realistic or not. I need to not be reminded of cancer when I'm not

---

[2] Jason Hoffman, "AYA Cancer Survivors More Likely to Have Mental Distress Than Healthy Individuals," *Oncology Nurse Advisor*, http://www.oncologynurseadvisor.com/side-effect-management/aya-cancer-survivors-at-higher-risk-for-mental-distress/article/574248

thinking about it. I need to not see an article about survival rates when I Google something else cancer-related. I need to be reassured that just because my anxiety and stress hasn't been diagnosed as a mental health issue, doesn't mean that it doesn't exist. I need to be able to talk to someone – even if it's just one person, even if they're not a therapist – about my experience. I need to have a coping strategy for when I'm worried about appointments or when fear of recurrence is getting to me. I need people around me who listen and try to understand, and who haven't forgotten that I had cancer.

A 2014 study investigated the needs of cancer survivors in terms of access to care; information; emotional, social and spiritual issues; physical issues, and economic and legal issues[3]. In the study, 44.6% of cancer survivors said that having someone to talk to when sadness overcame them was something that they needed, and 20.8% said that this need was not being met. 54.1% said that getting help for managing their concerns about the cancer coming back was a need, and 21.7% said this need was not being met. People are obviously struggling with coping with cancer and fear of recurrence, and many aren't getting any help with it.

What Needs To Change?

I believe we need more awareness of the emotional and mental difficulties after cancer. It would

[3] Berta M. Geller et al, "What are cancer survivors' needs and how well are they being met?", MDedge, https://www.mdedge.com/familymedicine/article/87617/oncology/what-are-cancer-survivors-needs-and-how-well-are-they-being

be great if cancer patients knew they might experience some stress even after cancer, and if they could know that this is completely normal and have their feelings validated. People need support when they are in distress, and they need to know from their medical team where they can go to get this support. This is especially true if a cancer survivor already has a mental health problem or is predisposed to having one. For example, a history of mental illness, a recurrence of cancer, or loss of independence when it comes to looking after themselves can all contribute to the risk of developing psychological distress after cancer.[4] Perhaps it would be helpful for a list such as the above table (or the entire list of all needs from that particular study) to be given to a cancer patient or survivor so that they can highlight the things that they need, and the medical team can help to provide it or direct them to appropriate support.

Talking About Cancer Survivorship

When I had my second and third cancer diagnoses in 2018, I wanted to let people at work know what was going on without it being awkward, and I wanted to let them know that it was fine for us to make light of it. However, throughout my whole cancer experience, from when my surgery drew closer to after I had recovered and was thinking of returning to work, I was torn between two approaches to cancer conversation: putting

---

[4] Christopher J. Recklitis et al, "Addressing Psychological Challenges After Cancer: A Guide for Clinical Practice," *Cancer Network*, https://www.cancernetwork.com/survivorship/addressing-psychological-challenges-after-cancer-guide-clinical-practice

on a brave face, showing how well I was and keeping my internal struggles to myself; or being honest about how scared I was and how hard recovering from surgery had been. In reality, I imagined that it didn't really matter because beyond "how are you?" I didn't think my colleagues would instigate a conversation about it unless I did. And there were few people I would typically want to talk to about it anyway.

I also struggle to know how much to talk about it with friends and family. Considering I was diagnosed with the third lot in May 2018 and it was removed in November 2018, I had six months of cancer being the biggest thing going on in my life, and everything else paled in comparison. It's longer than that if you add on the months of worrying about it before the diagnosis, and however many months I may continue to think about it and feel anxious about it after the event. That's a lot to be going on and it leaves little else for me to chat about. But I don't want to talk about myself all the time. I feel conscious of talking about myself too much and not listening to other people enough or talking about other things enough. I wanted to get the balance of conversation right.

Sometimes I want someone else to start the conversation, but unfortunately, it doesn't usually work out that way. After all, I look okay, my treatment is over – people think everything is back to normal now. So why would they bring up the subject of cancer if I don't? People aren't mind-readers and unless it's very obvious because of my mood or actions, they won't know anything is wrong unless I tell them. That means it's up to us as cancer survivors to keep the conversation going. As if we don't have enough to deal with, there's the responsibility of making other people aware of our emotional and mental health needs after cancer.

So how do we, as cancer survivors, talk about survivorship? Cancer chat doesn't have to be heavy all the time. Sometimes you can inject a little light-heartedness and humour. Take this email I sent around my work in 2018 as an example of my typical way of dealing with heavy subjects. I hoped my dark humour would set the tone and let people know that it's okay to talk about it and even make light of it:

Subject: Urgent: I am not adopting a baby goat

Hi all,

Just a quick note because I'm not sure how much everyone knows about me being randomly out of the office recently. I wish I could say it's because I've adopted a baby goat and it needs looking after, or Drake is on tour and as we're close friends he asked me to be his roadie, but the reality is much more mundane.

As some (many? all?!) of you know I have cancer (again, what a bore) which isn't ideal, to say the least. So I may continue to be in and out for the foreseeable future. Or out on a longer-term basis at some point in the future. Who knows? It's a magical mystery! Anyway, I'm getting it all sorted out (I should hope), and since I've done it before back in 2010, fairly sure everything's going to work out fine in the end.

I just wanted to make sure it's out in the open so we can all tease me for being a part-timer and/or mock cancer accordingly, as it rightly deserves.

Thanks for your understanding!

Sam

It would be a lot easier to talk about cancer if my scars were more visible. If my scars were on my hands, for example. And it would be easier to talk about the emotional effects of cancer if the mental scars were visible. I wrote about this in my short story "Wishes For Trauma", published in online literary magazine Degenerate Literature. If I was having a bad day the scar might look more red and inflamed, and people might ask about it. Or some days it would be barely visible at all. Maybe I could even command it to grow at my will, depending on whether I wanted to talk about things or whether I wanted to be left alone. It's very hard to talk about how you feel about cancer if all you really feel is sad that it happened. Sometimes I say I'm just feeling sorry for myself. Perhaps I am counting in my head all of the things I have lost. Fertility, my previous self-image, faith in my body, peace of mind. Even friends. Though I wouldn't name any names, there are a couple of friends who didn't get in touch with me after my second and third surgeries, who I had to reach out to myself, and one of them never did reply to my messages. I made as much effort as is reasonable to expect from me, and I didn't want to write him off. All I really wanted was a message to say he was thinking of me or to show that he was checking if I was still of this world. Even if he knew I was okay because he had looked at my social media, I wanted to hear from him because it showed that he knew and cared. I was disappointed and surprised when nine months after my hysterectomy I still hadn't heard from him, and I felt like I had lost someone who I would normally talk to about anything in the world, cancer being no exception. I had even gotten grief from him back in 2011 for not telling him until a year or so after the event that I'd had my bowel surgery due to cancer – and now here I was, trying to tell him about everything that had happened at the end of 2018, and show that I was okay, and he was nowhere to be found. They say that you find out who your real friends are at times like this (which is a bit of a corny cliché), but the confusing thing was that I knew he was a good friend before, and I didn't understand what had changed. Even my talk about how I don't like the battle language surrounding cancer doesn't really matter in this instance. There are a whole host of things you can say to a cancer patient that aren't particularly helpful – platitudes such as "you'll be fine", "you're so strong/brave, you can beat this", "just think positive", and so on. You don't know I'll be fine, I don't want the pressure of somehow having to "beat" this myself with my "strength", and I don't always feel like thinking positively. But I'd rather hear any of those than hear nothing at all from a friend. For the love of God, just say *something*.

Where to Talk About It

Websites and forums run by charities and other organisations can provide a great amount of support and sense of community for people with all kinds of illnesses. Communities can also be found on social media websites such as Twitter, and Facebook groups or pages. Twitter is a particularly good place to have conversations with other cancer survivors in an open way where other people are free to read or join in, and this is all part of continuing the conversation around cancer survivorship. Being honest with friends and family when you're having a bad day can also help to open up the conversation about how hard survivorship can sometimes be. Some people might understand better than others, and sometimes it might be awkward or difficult to bring it up, but you might sometimes find out that it's worth it if you give it a go. It might even bring you closer to a person.

Chapter Twelve
Self-Care For Cancer Survivors

A story has a beginning, a middle and an end, but this one isn't over. Cancer isn't a story that neatly finishes when treatment stops, as my thinning hair in early 2019 would have told you. That's why seven years after the first event, I was still thinking about seeing a therapist. By the time I did though, I wasn't really sure what I wanted out of it and I ended up feeling like it didn't work for me. How could it work if I didn't know what it working might look like? By that time, I had found ways to let out anything I needed to talk about, and I had developed some self-care rules to stick by. Here are a few self-care tips for cancer survivors that I have found work for me:

1. Find someone to talk to

I have found my circle after cancer to be very small. Few people know what is going on with my medical life at any given time, and even fewer who I talk to about how I feel about cancer. I've found that a couple of people have stopped talking to me since my most recent operations, which is very sad and surprising. But there are certain people who I can talk to about absolutely anything, and I take advantage of that. Not everyone will be receptive to cancer chat. Sometimes people feel awkward and don't know what to say. There have been times when trying to talk about parts of my cancer experience have made me feel more alone because the people I was talking to didn't understand where I was coming from. But there might be that one friend – or even more than one – who doesn't just let you talk about cancer, but who knows you well enough to notice when you're finding it hard to deal with being a cancer survivor, and who knows what you're going to say or what you're worried about before you say it. Having one person to talk to about it is better than keeping it all to yourself. It might even make the problem seem a little bit smaller than it did before.

Sometimes people make friends with other cancer patients during treatment. I never did – I wonder if it's something that tends to happen in the chemo lounge. But if you have friends who have also had cancer, they may be some of the best people to talk to, as they'll probably understand how you feel better than anyone else. Surround yourself with people who have stuck with you throughout your experience, and who you've always been able to lean on. This is your network of people who understand that it's never really over and that you still need them. They might be family or friends or people you chat to on the internet. Geographical proximity doesn't always mean emotional closeness.

2. See a therapist if you feel like you should

Don't wait around as long as I did to talk to a professional if that's what you think you want to do. Even if you're in two minds about it, you can still make the call and try one session. Counsellors often offer the first session as a sort of trial, so you won't be obligated to go back if you're not keen on it. And it's normal to have to try a couple of different counsellors before you find one that you're happy with. I wasn't offered any kind of counselling when I was diagnosed with bowel cancer, but the second and third time around I was asked if I wanted to speak to someone. I said no, because I didn't want to deal with it just then, and I knew from experience that I would probably feel worse about it when it was all over. But there's no harm in asking for more information so you can pursue help later if you want to. You might also want to see if there are any support groups in your area that you could join.

3. Use the internet...

I have found the internet to be a great resource for talking about cancer and finding people in similar situations. I've listed some good websites to have a look at in the appendix, including charity websites and forums. For example, when I first got my stoma, the Ileostomy Association forum was invaluable to me in terms of finding out if my experiences were normal and hearing from people in the same situation – including people who'd had their colostomies or internal pouches for years and were practically experts. If you're active on social media, you'll find lots of support there, too. There is a Lynch syndrome support group on Facebook and plenty of people blogging and talking about cancer on Twitter. I didn't use the internet so much while everything was happening, but I liked to read about other people's survivorship experiences afterwards and hear that other people have similar feelings to me long after their treatment has ended.

4. ...But not all the time!

This may seem like a bit of a contradiction, but as well as being a great place to get support, the internet can also be scary. You'll know this if you've ever Googled a seemingly benign medical symptom only to find an article that says the condition in question might kill you. If you have someone else in your family who is happy to research, let them do it for you. Peter and Chris would both research a variety of things about my condition without me ever asking, so when I went to talk to them about something that was worrying me, they already had the answers. Half the time when I did Google something about Whipple procedure, Google would tell me that people also ask the question "What is the life expectancy after a Whipple procedure?" Well, thanks, Google. I wasn't really thinking about that until just now. So I'd suggest using the internet to find support, but not to find answers to medical questions quite so much – that's what doctors are for. Always proceed with caution, and if you're reading something that's making you feel worried or anxious, recognise when it's time to close down your browser and do something a little less scary.

5. Write about how you feel

In place of having someone to talk to, or as an excellent addition, I'd recommend writing. You don't have to be Shakespeare to write down what you're thinking, and the act of doing so might make you feel better. I have people that I talk to but I write poetry and blog posts and random thoughts anyway because it's what I've always done. If you create something you're happy with, it's also nice to see that something good can come out of feeling bad. Of course, I'm not saying that it's worth going through cancer and the trauma it brings if it means you can write a great poem. But I have written many things I am happy with that stemmed from this subject, and writing – or making any other art, for that matter – is a great outlet. I also love to share my story by writing guest blog posts and articles for other websites. It's a good way to contribute to a community and connect with other cancer survivors. Writing poetry and stories to submit to literary magazines is another great outlet, and brings the world of cancer survivorship and the issues around it to a potentially new audience.

6. Be kind to yourself

It's easy to ask too much of ourselves as cancer survivors. For one thing, apparently we should be happy when treatment is over because we can get back to our normal lives. But we know it doesn't really happen that way. Maybe we see a news article about a cancer survivor climbing Mount Everest to raise money for charity and think we should be doing something similar instead of simply trying to get back to normal. Or perhaps we think that cancer should have made us braver, stronger, or more grateful for life, and we don't think we've changed enough. But you don't have to be happy all the time just because the cancer is gone – you're only human if you're still upset by what happened in the past, if you're worried might happen in the future, and if you're anxious about follow-up appointments. And if you want to set yourself a big physical challenge or raise money for charity, that's great, but it's not an obligation for everyone. If you don't feel like cancer has changed you for the better, that's okay, too – it's cancer. It's absolutely horrendous and the fact that you've even gotten this far is enough. Don't be hard on yourself if you think you're not living up to the media or society's idea of what a cancer survivor should be. You're doing just fine. In fact, you should celebrate when you can, and if you want to. Celebrate your cancerversary – however many years of being cancer-free. Celebrate a clean scan or a positive appointment. There is so much bad that comes with a cancer diagnosis. it's okay to celebrate small victories.

7. Don't treat your body like it's the enemy

As I mentioned in an earlier chapter, I spent a lot of time thinking of my body like it was some evil entity somehow separate from myself. I think I did this to distance myself from a body that no longer felt normal to me. Our bodies form part of our identities and when they change during and after cancer, it can feel like our identities have changed. Or maybe I was trying to distance myself from the body, which was to blame, so that I could feel like getting cancer wasn't my fault (which of course it wasn't, anyway). Plus, saying "something is wrong with me" feels more threatening and immediate than "something is wrong with my body", which sounds more distant and might also be why I disconnected with my body a little.

This feeling of disconnect was reinforced by the way I was thinking and this wasn't healthy or helpful to me. So extend the same kindness to your body as you do to your mind, or as you would to a friend who has cancer. It's normal to feel betrayed by your body and to lose your trust in it. But remember that cancer is the enemy, and it's not your fault or your body's. Your body is you. Think about all the things you like about it. Look after it. If you need to change your thinking patterns in order to reframe the problem back to cancer and not your body, listen to your thoughts and identify the words that seem unfair to your body. Make an effort to actively change your thoughts. You'll feel better once you realise that your body isn't out to get you and it's still very much part of you. And finally, if you feel you need to, tell your body that you forgive it. Wipe the slate clean, and reclaim ownership. Your body is you, and it's on your side.

8. Avoid cancery things when you need to

Cancery things. You know: charity adverts, coffee mornings, fun runs, fundraising television programmes, Facebook groups. Sometimes it feels like cancer is everywhere and you can't get away from it. While all of these things tend to be run by charities and are for the greater good, you don't have to engage with them if you're not feeling up to it. If you feel like hearing about cancer is going to upset you, make you feel nervous about an upcoming appointment, or remind you of all the things that happened to you, then turn off the television, or decline the event invitation. I once booked a day off work because I knew that day we were hosting a Macmillan coffee morning. I had been doing quite well not thinking about cancer and I wanted to continue that. I've also been known to unfriend people on Facebook who post lots of images that say things like "Share this ribbon to support those affected by cancer." These posts don't actually help anyone in any practical way, and I just found them annoying and upsetting – a constant reminder of my illness. I didn't want to see them, so I took action. You might even find that people you spend time with talk about cancer occasionally, and not in the context of yourself – they might know someone else or talk about a celebrity who has cancer. It's okay to excuse yourself and come back a few minutes later when the topic of conversation has changed. It's not selfish to not want to hear about someone else's illness when you're still struggling to deal with your own.

9. Choose to go to your appointments

The NHS is brilliant as far as I'm concerned and if you've had cancer you're likely to be checked up on fairly regularly. Appointments are scary – the anticipation of going, the sitting in the waiting room, the having the test done or talking to the consultant, the waiting for the results of the tests. But it's worth going through the anxiety and keeping an eye on things. Remember Mr Doshi sending me for that hysteroscopy? One appointment could be the difference between finding cancer early and treating it or finding it too late. Plus, if the tests all come back fine, then that's peace of mind you can rely on. It's better to go through "scanxiety" than not go at all. And I say this has someone who earlier today thought "My CT scan was a couple of weeks ago so I should be getting a letter soon... unless I don't get a letter. What if they call me instead and say they need to make an appointment with my consultant to discuss the results because something isn't right? Because it's come back?" And my stomach falls through the floor. But I put it out of my mind, think of something else – until next time, at least. The fear is still better than the alternative.

It can also be useful to remember that we always have a choice about whether we go to appointments, as that can give us a feeling of control. Yes, you should go to your appointments, but when you do go, you are choosing to go and do the best thing for your body. You have control over that decision.

10. Be vigilant

This ties in with going to your appointments, but it's about going a little further than that. Being worried about our bodies is a defence mechanism. It's our brains trying to help us survive. We might call it paranoia or hypochondria, and it might feel terrible worrying about every little thing we notice about our bodies, but we're just being vigilant. Follow through with that vigilance by talking to your GP or consultant about whatever is worrying you. Whether it's a headache, a new lump or bump or rash or weird pain, it's much better to get it checked out than to live with the worry – or to leave it and let it get worse, if it is something that needs to be dealt with.

11. Give yourself worry time

Another tip I've heard is to set aside a time for worrying. I haven't tried it much myself but it sounds useful - every time you start to worry, tell yourself to save it for your scheduled worry time. Then, allow yourself to spend 20 minutes or so thinking about what's worrying you, writing it down, talking about it or whatever helps, and then when the 20 minutes is up, put it away until your worry time the next day. It's meant to reduce the time you spend worrying during the day, without meaning you bottle things up or suppress them completely.

12. Remember that thoughts aren't facts

I first read this excellent piece of advice in *The Cancer Survivor's Companion: Practical ways to cope with your feelings* by Lucy Atkins and Dr Frances Goodhart. It simply means that just because a thought springs into your head, doesn't mean that you have to believe it or trust it. For example, if you're waiting for an appointment and the date is sooner than you expected, you might think *oh no, they want to see me next week so it must be bad news.* That's just a thought, and it may not be the case at all. You just don't know. Don't treat every worry that comes into your head as a true fact. It's just something that you've come up with yourself and doesn't have any bearing on the actual outcome. (Also, I've found that it's very difficult to second-guess the NHS. Why are appointments set for when they are? I've been both right and wrong before trying to figure out what it all means.)

***

I am lucky that my fear and anxiety hasn't turned into depression or PTSD. I usually cope fairly well with my emotional problems, and when I don't, I write them out. But when I was recovering from my hysterectomy, and again when I was recovering from my Whipple surgery, I felt like my problems were never going to end. 2018 was just one thing after another in terms of diagnoses, setbacks and symptoms, and my recovery from the surgeries took so long and was so emotionally draining that I couldn't see a light at the end of the tunnel. I am so far away from that now and I am in disbelief about how far I have come, but it just shows how easily everything can go wrong. It feels like I am never that far away from being back there. All it takes is one appointment, one biopsy, one set of bad results. I feel like I am always on my guard for it, but even trying to be prepared for bad news doesn't make it any easier when it comes along. There is no real end to this story. I am still a little scared and waiting for the next diagnosis, but I am trying to enjoy life as much as possible in the meantime. That's my reality of being a cancer survivor.

Acknowledgements

Thank you to Peter – my rock, my love, and my source of logical, practical reason when I am lost. Thank you to my parents for their constant support. And my family – Karen, Neil, Brandon, Jade, Stella, Michelle. Everyone who came to see me in hospital and at home. Thank you to Chris, my best friend who I couldn't be without. Thank you to my girls – Rachael, Emma, Zoe and Jess for visiting me, distracting me, sending me wonderful gifts, and of course for years of friendship and memories. Thank you to Peter's family and friends for supporting both of us, and to our good friend Ian. Thank you to my colleagues for your understanding, support and friendship. You made sure I didn't have anything to worry about at work on top of everything else. Thank you to my medical team – Dr Khan, Mr Rashed, Mr Doshi, Miss Biswas, Mr Davies, Dr Das, Dr Kadri, Mr Bhardwaj, and all of the staff who looked after me at Kettering General Hospital, Northampton General Hospital, Leicester Royal Infirmary and Leicester General Hospital. You are a credit to the NHS and I wouldn't be here without you.

Thank you to You&Me - America's Medical Magazine (www.youandmemagazine.com) for publishing my story "The Tissue Room" in 2016, which was subsequently used in this book. Thank you also to Elephants and Tea (elephantsandtea.com) and Womb Cancer Support UK (wombcancersupportuk.weebly.com) for publishing my guest blog posts which were excerpts of this book. My poem "Iceland" was originally published in Ethel Zine Volume 5 in February 2020.

Appendix
(I might not have one, but this book should)

The below websites and books are all sources that I have used and found helpful:

bethgainer.com: A personal blog about breast cancer and health advocacy.

bowelcanceruk.org: UK bowel cancer charity

The Cancer Survivor's Companion: Practical ways to cope with your feelings by Lucy Atkins and Dr Frances Goodhart

cansurround.com: A place for cancer patients and survivors to journal their thoughts, try relaxation exercises and get support.

doesthedogdie.com: Find out whether a movie or TV series features a character with cancer (as well as a wide variety of other plot points such as the death of various animals, sexual assault, seizures, eating disorders and more) so you can decide whether or not you want to watch it.

iasupport.org: Ileostomy and internal pouch information and support.

ihadcancer.com: Social network for cancer survivors, with community chat, blogs and private messaging.

livebetterwithmenopause.com: Useful information and gift ideas for women going through the menopause.

macmillan.org.uk: Cancer support, information and community.

nancyspoint.com: A personal blog about breast cancer and loss.

pancreaticcancer.org.uk: Features useful patient stories about recovering from Whipple surgery.

stupidcancer.org: Help and support for young adults with cancer.

.

Printed in Great Britain
by Amazon